CREATING EFFECTIVE RULES IN
PUBLIC SECTOR ORGANIZATIONS

Creating Effective Rules in Public Sector Organizations

LEISHA DEHART-DAVIS

GEORGETOWN UNIVERSITY PRESS / WASHINGTON, DC

The publisher is not responsible for third-party websites or their content. URL links were active at time of publication.

Library of Congress Cataloging-in-Publication Data

Names: DeHart-Davis, Leisha, author.
Title: Creating effective rules in public sector organizations / Leisha Dehart-Davis.
Other titles: Public management and change.
Description: Washington, DC : Georgetown University Press, 2017. | Series: Public management and change series
Identifiers: LCCN 2016037923 (print) | LCCN 2016057543 (ebook) | ISBN 9781626164468 (hbk : alk. paper) | ISBN 9781626164475 (pbk : alk. paper) | ISBN 9781626164482 (ebk)
Subjects: LCSH: Organizational behavior—Management. | Employee rules.
Classification: LCC HD58.7 .D44 2017 (print) | LCC HD58.7 (ebook) | DDC 352.6/7—dc23
LC record available at https://lccn.loc.gov/2016037923

♾ This book is printed on acid-free paper meeting the requirements of the American National Standard for Permanence in Paper for Printed Library Materials.

18 17   9 8 7 6 5 4 3 2 First printing

Printed in the United States of America

Cover design by N. Putens.

To H. Allen Davis, who is Superman, Mr. Mom,
and Top Chef rolled into one incredible husband.

CONTENTS

ILLUSTRATIONS

Figures

Tables

Boxes

ACKNOWLEDGMENTS

The idea of a solo-authored book is a misnomer and *Creating Effective Rules in Public Sector Organizations* is no exception. The following people have been instrumental in its development, although the book's flaws are mine alone.

Beryl Radin, editor of the Public Management and Change Series, and Donald Jacobs, at Georgetown University Press, gave this book a chance and recruited two tough reviewers whose commentary vastly improved the quality of the manuscript.

Many University of Kansas people played a formative role in the development of this book. The School of Public Affairs and Administration gave me a research intensive semester, a sabbatical, and grant funding. Steven Maynard-Moody pressed his street-level bureaucracy students into service; they conducted interviews and faithfully transcribed them. Steven also provided resources for the research from the Institute for Policy and Social Research. John Nalbandian and Ray Hummert helped me secure access to local government organizations. Marilu Goodyear served as perpetual champion of the green tape concept; George Frederickson encouraged its development. Randy Davis and Erin Borry were instrumental in conducting the Local Government Workplaces Study and carved honors-winning dissertations out of its data. Erin also patiently assured me that she would finish the book were I to be hit by a bus. As a doctoral student at KU, Nate Wright worked with me on a very difficult interview process in one location; that he and I both survived is a testament to his resilience. The undergraduate research assistants who executed the details of this research are making their marks on the world: Hilary Badger, Chris Engel, Tawnya Metzler, and Nick Shigouri.

The University of North Carolina School of Government, my most recent academic home, is one of the few places on earth where engaged research is welcomed and appreciated and where both formal and practical knowledge flourish side-by-side. In support of this book, Tom Thornburg provided administrative counsel; Trey Allen and Jeff Welty guided me on HB2; Bill Rivenbark and Norma Houston gave practical examples of rules; and Diane Juffras and Drake Maynard provided legal review. The Local Government Research Collaborative funded the research on which chapter 4 is based; thank you to David Swindell, Karen Thoreson, Toni Shope, and members of the collaborative for making that happen. Daniel Irvin and Esther Lee contributed painstaking citation research.

Many excellent public administration colleagues generously reviewed chapters and provided critical feedback, including Sanjay Pandey, Zach Oberfield, and Erin Borry, all on whose work I rely heavily; Wesley Kaufmann, Lars Tummers, and Cullen Merritt, who make research fun and thought provoking; Jessica Sherrod and Benjamin Brunjes, who prove that doctoral students are the toughest critics. Shannon Portillo conducted interviews, reviewed a book chapter, and (more important) provided insights from her own critical research. Rosemary O'Leary and Cam Stivers provided intellectual guidance and support. David Brown reviewed chapter 5 from a police perspective, expanding my perspective on the Five-Second Rule.

Most important, my family made this book possible. Sydney DeHart Davis and Dayton Herlong Davis have been patient and steadfast supporters (especially given that they are teenagers), enduring my sabbatical from domestic duties this past year. The book owes its existence to H. Allen Davis, who has made this book, and our life, possible.

For the local government managers who sponsored this research because they wanted to hear their employees' voices: you labor with the angels. I cannot name you (due to confidentiality requirements of institutional review boards) but you demonstrate Pericles's sentiment that all good things of this earth flow into the city.

INTRODUCTION

Organizational rules are indispensable to public management. Through rules, public managers hire and promote employees, purchase equipment and supplies with taxpayer dollars, resolve internal conflicts between employees and supervisors, formulate budgets, and standardize work activities. Public employees also use rules to engage with citizens, deliver public goods and services, and manage their workloads. Beyond the nuts and bolts, rules structure the relationship between public organizations and employees, setting behavioral expectations and signaling an organization's culture. The list is not exhaustive but illustrative: rules enable public organizations to function in ways that would be impossible without them.

Despite the indispensability of organizational rules to public management, most practical and scholarly literature tends to focus on the negative effects of rules (Goodsell 2000). Reformers seeking to reinvent government assume that rules make for sluggish bureaucracies, stifle employee creativity, foster inefficiency, breed rigid bureaucratic behavior, and dim hopes of organizational effectiveness (Cohen and Brand 1993; US National Performance Review 1993; Cohen and Eimicke 1998; Osborne and Plastrik 2000; Osborne and Gaebler 1992). Scholars make similar generalizations, assuming that rules dampen employee morale, fracture workplace relationships, and create red tape (see Adler and Borys 1996 for an overview). Both of these perspectives assume that slashing rules creates happier workforces, greater operational efficiencies, and stronger organizational performance.

While these criticisms sometimes hold true—who among us has not encountered a bad rule?—focusing on the pathological aspects of rules yields a lopsided and incomplete portrait of reality. Negative rule conceptions limit our ability to prescribe solutions and narrow the education we pass down to generations of managers and scholars in public administration graduate programs. Consequently, public administration scholars and practitioners alike lack a comprehensive understanding of the organization rule and its role in public organizations.

Also missing from scholarly thinking is the realization that organizational rules reflect contemporary issues of public administration. For example, workplace drug-testing policies in states with legalized recreational marijuana reflect tensions created by federalism, which emerge from the conflict between state and federal law (Cherminsky et al. 2015). Police restraint procedures convey assumptions about civil rights and the (in)appropriate use of force. Volunteer policies imply appropriate roles of citizens in co-production. These are not tiny issues: whether these rules function well or fail miserably affects the lives of everyday citizens. Understanding effective rule functioning is vital to the field of public administration.

To create a more comprehensive understanding of public sector rules, this book consolidates theory and evidence in a framework of three interrelated perspectives: organizational, individual, and behavioral (see Figure I.1). The organizational perspective magnifies specific rule functions that enable organizations to pursue rational, goal-oriented action. The individual perspective illuminates how public employees experience rules as messages conveyed about the true nature of the public organization and the place of the individual within it. The behavioral perspective focuses on how public employees act upon rules. Rules require followers, and followers are not mindless cogs in a bureaucratic wheel; they engage in a variety of cooperative and uncooperative rule behaviors, from straightforward rule compliance to prosocial rule-bending.

In drawing on three perspectives to portray organizational rules, this book uses an analytical eclecticism approach, which is a type of knowledge integration that "connects different knowledge sources about one particular topic" (Raadschelders 2011, 191). Analytical eclecticism seeks to solve particular problems by drawing across academic research traditions to gain pragmatic knowledge that embraces complexity and generates flexible frameworks for organizing that knowledge. Analytical eclecticism seeks to overcome the tunnel vision of disciplinary social science research, which risks incorrect conclusions by focusing on certain explanatory factors to the exclusion of others and contributes to an incomplete picture of social phenomena (Sil and Katzenstein 2011). This is not to say that disciplinary research is marginalized. On the contrary, analytical eclecticism relies on disciplinary research for the depth and focus it brings to particular areas of study.

In keeping with analytical eclecticism, the organizational rules framework draws on theory and evidence gathered across geographic, historic, and disciplinary settings. The framework is based on data collected in the contemporary

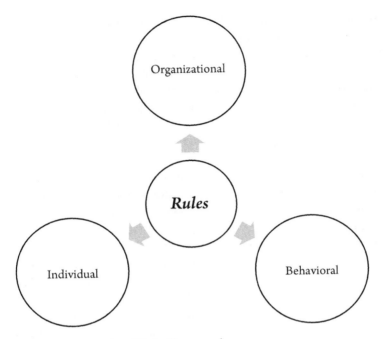

Figure I.1 The Organizational Rules Framework

US local government context but also draws on research in public and private sectors at all levels of government and around the globe, including in locales in Germany, Denmark, the Netherlands, Great Britain, France, and China. From a historical perspective, nearly all rules research originates with Max Weber, the early twentieth-century German sociologist who featured rules in his pathbreaking description of bureaucracy in the United States and Prussia. After Weber, the intellectual trail splinters off, entangling sociologists, social psychologists, organization theorists and behaviorists, law and society researchers, political scientists, economists, and (last but not least) public management scholars. The framework thus casts a broad net of theory and evidence and promises findings that should easily generalize across settings (although only time and comparative research will tell).

The use of multiple perspectives to convey a comprehensive view of organizational rules does not imply mutually exclusive categories; it merely allows the reader to put on a different pair of lenses for viewing those rules. The organizational perspective assumes the vantage point of public sector managers; the individual perspective focuses on the public employee; the behavioral perspective examines how rules can be acted upon by members of public organizations. Each perspective is alone insufficient because rules are inherently social constructs: rules create relationships between people and organizations and yield behaviors that either serve or undermine organizational purposes.

Another point of clarification about the organizational rules framework is the distinction between individual and behavioral perspectives. This distinction might strike some readers as false. After all, organization behavior researchers study individuals and groups within organizations, including their perceptions, attitudes, and actions (Robbins and Judge 2016). By contrast, the framework separates individual and behavioral perspectives because how rules are experienced and how they are acted upon are different topics. The difference between rules as experiences and rules as behaviors arises in the voices of the local government employees interviewed for this book, as well as in the multidisciplinary literature on organizational rules.

Before delving into the organizational rules framework, some groundwork is necessary for understanding rules as both organization and administration phenomena. First is a consideration of the contemporary context of public organizations as illustrated by a controversial North Carolina law that requires public bathrooms and facilities to be designated based on birth certificate sex rather than gender identity. Next, public organizational rules are justified as a topic worthy of stand-alone attention, particularly in light of the extensive and rich literature on private organizational rules within sociology and organizational behavior. Organizational rules are then differentiated from other organization structures and behaviors with which they can be conflated. Finally, rules are placed within the context of relevant public administration theories. The focus then turns to the research on which the book is based and lays the groundwork for the chapters ahead.

The Contemporary Context of Public Organizations

Public organizations are creatures of their political, economic, and social environments. To illustrate, consider the current controversy in the State of North Carolina, where the governor has signed into law the Public Facilities Privacy and Security Act (S.L. 2016-3/HB2, also known as HB2).[1] The law requires (among other things) that public schools, government agencies, and public college campuses assign multi-occupancy bathrooms and changing facilities based on biological sex rather than gender identity.[2] The law thus requires transgender people who have not surgically changed sex to use the restroom of the sex that is opposite to that with which they identify.[3]

HB2 derives from the ultimate political battle between a conservative state general assembly and more liberal urban city centers. It was triggered by the passage of an amendment to the City of Charlotte's antidiscrimination ordinance, which added protections against discrimination for lesbian, gay, bisexual, and transgendered (LGBT) people.[4] (Interestingly, the revised ordinance makes no mention of restrooms.) Unhappy with the affront to state power (North Carolina does not have the "home rule" that would allow cities and counties to formulate ordinances that contradict state law), the North Carolina General Assembly called legislators back to a special session to address the Charlotte ordinance. Opponents viewed the ordinance as an assault on privacy rights and an overreach of local government authority. That special session produced HB2, which, along with requiring the users of restroom and changing facilities to adhere to distinctions based on their biological sex at birth, invalidated all LGBT antidiscrimination ordinances and omitted LGBT as a protected category of people. Thus HB2 can be understood as a power struggle between conservative and liberal, state and local, and urban and rural interests. Adding fuel to the fire, HB2 is being challenged in federal court; the state's democratic attorney general has vowed not to defend the law; the US Justice Department has deemed HB2 a violation of Title VII of the Civil Rights Act of 1964 and threatened the state's federal education funding; and the Obama administration has issued guidance requiring public schools to make bathrooms available based on gender identity rather than sex.

HB2 is socially rooted in a culture war between conservative and liberal worldviews. To illustrate the divide, 2015 Gallup opinion polling suggests that 58 percent of Americans believe that same-sex marriage should be legal, an increase from 27 percent a little over a decade ago. But 40 percent oppose it.[5] North Carolina's local government organizations and state agencies are caught in this societal tug-of-war between those who view transgender bathroom users as a threat to family values, privacy, and public safety and those who view the law as an assault on the civil rights of LGBT people.

The economic backdrop of HB2 emerges as North Carolina faces a dramatic loss in business from economic boycotts of the state. As of this writing, 160 corporate leaders have signed an open letter calling for the law's repeal; five states, eighteen cities, three counties, and the District of Columbia have banned public funding for travel to North Carolina;[6] the United Kingdom has issued a travel warning for LGBT people going to North Carolina;[7] and Bruce Springsteen, Pearl Jam, and Maroon 5 have canceled concerts in the state. In an effort to slow the economic hemorrhage, North Carolina governor Pat McCrory has issued an executive order adding sexual orientation and gender identity as protected classes of employees (which were not previously identified as such).[8]

It is unclear whether or if any organizational rules will emerge as a result of

HB2.[9] Making the strong assumption that the law survives court challenges, HB2 will most likely generate implementation guidance to state agencies and local governments that could center on the need to provide both single- and multiple-occupancy restrooms. However, Margaret Spellings, the president of the University of North Carolina system, has stated that she has "no intent to exercise my authority to promulgate any guidelines or regulations that require that transgender students use the restrooms consistent with their biological sex."[10] The refusal to craft organizational rules can be a powerful symbol of bureaucratic resistance.

HB2 adeptly illustrates the complex environment in which public organizations function. Pulled by political winds, shaped by societal norms, and constrained by economic forces, public organizations are subject to a distinct set of environmental pressures. While private organizations can experience some of these same pressures, public organizations are explicitly and intentionally shaped by them but with less room to maneuver. A more narrow focus on the legal, economic, and normative differences between public and private organizations shows that public organizational rules merit separate study.

The Case for Studying Rules in Public Organizations

Even with a distinct set of environmental pressures, should public organizations be studied as a stand-alone topic? The question is valid, given the wealth of research on private sector organizational rules. The answer is yes, based on two differences between public and private organizational rules: distinct legal and economic structures produce more rules—and different rules—for public organizations; and public organizations are expected to serve public values. While private organizations can choose to adopt public values, or may be required to do so by government regulation, there is generally no societal or cultural indication that they voluntarily do so. Thus public organizational rules become freighted with meaning and intentionally or implicitly convey the values of the state.

More Rules, Different Rules

Many rules in public organizations are rooted in law, whether they derive from constitutional, legislative, judicial, or regulatory sources. Court interpretations of the US Constitution trigger public organizational rules that protect public employee speech, limit employee drug testing, and guarantee employee due process before termination. Adjudicatory decisions by federal and state administrative law judges influence organizational rules that grant environmental permits, distribute welfare benefits, and pursue workforce diversity (O'Leary

1994; Rosenbloom and O'Leary 1997). Federal, state, and local regulations govern public organizational rules on purchasing, records retention, domestic partner benefits, and the allowable scope of public services, to name just a few. The private sector does not contend with similar legal constraints on their daily operations.

But law is not the only difference between public and private organizational rules. Public organizations are also thought to have more rules than private organizations because they are subject to greater political control (Wilson 1989, 242; Bozeman, Reed, and Scott 1992). From city councils to congressional appropriations committees, elected officials pull purse strings with leverage over organizational machinery. Diverse stakeholders impose competing interests and multiply procedural requirements (Kaufman 1977). For example, county health departments are procedurally responsive to the needs of the state health and human services agency, to citizen-patients, and to their governing boards, to name just a few. Political scientist James Q. Wilson puts a Machiavellian spin on it when he juxtaposes the decline of patronage against the expansion of governmental activity to produce a keen interest by politicos in creating rules that hamstring federal agencies (1989). While private organizations are subject to some external control—by regulatory agencies and government funders, for example (Bozeman 1987)—political control of public organizations is generally more intense and confining.

Goal ambiguity provides another explanation for differences in public and private organizational rules (Rainey, Pandey, and Bozeman 1995). Unlike public organizations, private firms seek to maximize profit, which creates constant pressure to deliver goods and services more efficiently (Bozeman, Reed, and Scott 1992). Profit is a clear performance indicator that allows private sector performance to be compared across different types of firms. By contrast, public organizations address wicked problems with complex roots, uncertain solutions, and unmeasurable goals (Head and Alford 2008). Without an easy way to demonstrate accomplishment and no bottom line to strengthen, public organizations substitute rules and compliance and in the process become more rule-bound than private organizations (Lan and Rainey 1992).[11] Goal ambiguity also can encourage individual public managers to amass budgetary resources to demonstrate personal power, possibly using rules to do so (Rainey, Pandey, and Bozeman 1995).

It's unclear whether public organizations have more rules than private firms because the empirical evidence is mixed. On balance, public organizations appear to have greater rule orientation than private ones (Boyne 2002). This conclusion masks considerable variance in study results and measures, however.

To illustrate, Lan and Rainey found no differences in procedures or rule violation checks between 120 public and private organizations in Syracuse, New York, but they did find higher levels of unnecessary rules in public organizations than in their private-sector counterparts (2002). In contrast with conventional wisdom, private sector managers in Bruce Buchanan's 1975 study perceived organizational structure (including rule orientation) to be more important in their organizations than public managers believed. The Aston Study found no public-private differences in formal paperwork but more personnel procedures in public organizations (Pugh et al. 1968). Across studies, public managers perceive higher red tape on average than their private-sector counterparts (Bozeman and Feeney 2011, 74), although the magnitude of these differences varies considerably (Boyne 2002, 112).

At the end of the day, actual sectoral differences matter less than the popular belief that public organizations have more rules. The latter produces greater scrutiny and less benefit of the doubt for public organizations by media, citizens, and politicians. A more comprehensive understanding of rules in public organizations could help overcome this bias and enable scholars to better educate public managers for more effective organizational functioning.

Public Values

Public and private organizational rules also differ in how they symbolize public values (Van Wart 1998, 15). Public values are defined as the "normative consensus about the principles on which governments and policies should be based" (Bozeman 2007, 36). This is not to say that private organizations cannot voluntarily pursue public values (Jørgensen and Bozeman 2007, 374) nor that they are regulated into doing so. Rather, society *expects* public organizations to represent public values in all they say and do, including through their rules (Geuras and Garofalo 2005, 17). To assess the difference, public management scholar Zeger Van der Wal and his colleagues surveyed the values of 766 public and private managers in the Netherlands (Van der Wal, De Graaf, and Lasthuizen 2008). The researchers found that accountability, lawfulness, and incorruptibility rank as the top three values for public managers, while profitability, accountability, and reliability rank as the top three values among private managers. (Among private managers, lawfulness—acting in accordance with laws and rules—didn't even make the top ten.)

Organizational rules symbolize public values through form and function. Rules enable efficiency, equity, and accountability—three frequently cited public values. Efficiency, a free market principle that maximizes profits by minimizing the ratio of inputs to outputs, allows public organizations to be careful stewards of taxpayer dollars. Rules enable efficiency by coordinating individual and group action in the service of organizational goals (the "sheet music" effect). Equity, a value decidedly *not* associated with free markets, pertains to the distribution of goods and services regardless of individual recipient characteristics such as race, gender, or income.[12] The written form of organizational rules facilitates equity by subjecting all to its precepts: rules available in black and white apply equally to frontline employees and department heads, high performers and slackers alike. Accountability is a public value particularly important in an era of deep distrust of government. Within public organizations, rules enable accountability by articulating the responsibilities and rights of employees.

Public organizational rules can also symbolize values well beyond equity, efficiency, and accountability. Table I.1 identifies the public values associated with five common local government rules, as drawn from the public values inventory devised by public management scholars Torben Jørgensen and Barry Bozeman (2007). Capital reserve fund policies seek financial stewardship, while complaint processes strive for responsiveness to citizens. Due process protects

Table I.1 Public Service Values of Five Common Local Government Rules

Organizational Rule	Public Service Values
Capital reserve fund policies, which set aside increments of money to be used for capital improvements	Financial stewardship, rationality
Due process rules that require just or reasonable cause to impose adverse employee actions (demotion, suspension, termination), along with impartial hearing with advance notice	Individual rights, fairness, equity, neutrality, respect, antidiscrimination
Ethics policies, e.g., avoiding conflicts of interest, acting impartially, shunning private gain	Professionalism, honesty, moral standards, ethical consciousness, integrity, safeguarding against abuse of power
Complaint processes that require documentation and response to issues and concerns raised by individual citizens	Responsiveness, performance, accountability, transparency
Public records rules that specify how long and what types of records must be kept and when which records can be destroyed	Transparency, accountability, knowledge, historical preservation, legalism

Note: Public service values come from Torben Beck Jørgensen and Barry Bozeman, "Public Values: An Inventory," *Administration and Society* 39, no. 3 (2007): 354–81.

public employees from arbitrary and capricious managerial action, whereas public records ensure historical preservation. Ethics policies seek to elicit public values that encourage certain behaviors (integrity and professionalism) and discourage others (dishonesty and abuse of power). While these rules vary widely in content, they share the appearance of seeking specific public values.

There are limits to the argument that public organizational rules symbolize public values. Rules can be inefficient, inequitable, and obfuscating (Brodkin and Majmundar 2010). Rules can deliberately ignore, circumvent, or sabotage public values. Rules can impose value tradeoffs, such as the welfare requirements that pit compassion against fraud prevention or financial stewardship against the social safety net (Moynihan and Herd 2010). Rules reveal the values of the state and often (but not always) serve the public good. These limits notwithstanding, rules weave public values into the fabric of public organizations and help justify the study of rules in public organizations as a stand-alone topic.

The Organizational Rule: What It Is and What It Is Not

Organizational rules are written requirements for specific behaviors under particular circumstances.[13] In defining rules this way we will cover a good deal of conceptual territory but exclude other phenomena in the process.[14] Within organizations, rules can be standard operating procedures, policies, or guidelines. Outside the organization, rules can be laws, ordinances, regulations, common law, court rulings, and administrative law decisions, all of which can influence the formulation of organizational rules. But these are not organizational rules in themselves. Rules can be communicated through a variety of means — memoranda, manuals, verbal communications, emails — but these are not rules either; they are only the conduits for disseminating rules. Finally, it is easy to conflate rules with other forms of an organization's structure, such as formalization, centralization, and hierarchy, as well as with patterns such as routines, practices, norms, and unwritten rules. While these concepts have implications for organizational rules, they are distinct concepts to be discussed separately.

Rules vs. Other Forms of Organizational Structure

Structure is the social architecture that arranges individuals and groups in organizations and delineates relationships between them (Tolbert and Hall 2009, 20; Hall 1999, 47). Structure is formal, meaning it is explicitly developed and sanctioned by the organization. Scholars commonly reference three types of structure: formalization, or the extent of written organizational materials; centralization, or the upward locus of power; and complexity, or the hierarchical layers and departmental specializations (Aiken and Hage 1966; Pugh et al. 1968; Hall 1963; Rainey 2014, 217).

Intuition suggests that formalization, centralization, and hierarchy go hand in hand and result in quintessential bureaucracy.[15] However, the scholarly evidence is not so clear. Hierarchical organizations can be decentralized and centralized organizations can have flat organization structures (Donaldson 2001, 25; Harris and Raviv 2002). An organization can be decentralized and flat while having more rules and documentation, presumably due to the "remote control" delegation function of rules, as sociologist Alvin Gouldner has called it (1954). Consider an academic research center with thirty employees and one director. The center has only two layers of staff but a highly centralized structure in which the director makes all the decisions. Thus, flat structures are not necessarily more decentralized nor are hierarchical structures more centralized.

It makes sense that formalization, centralization, and hierarchy do not necessarily converge when considering the role of individual power in each form of structure. Where centralization and hierarchy assign power to individual organization members, formalization and rules restrain power and render all individuals within the organization subject to its precepts (Weber 1978, 983).[16] If rules truly level the organizational playing field, rules can also peacefully coexist with empowered employees and fewer layers of authority. The proposition is not formulaic, as some public organizations can be high in all three forms of structure. But it does contradict stereotypical notions of bureaucracy fed by conventional wisdom. Rules and routines and norms and practices are behaviors that can incorrectly appear similar to the untrained eye.

Rules vs. Routines, Norms, and Practices

Rules are different from routines, norms, and practices, but they overlap enough in content to require clarification. One difference lies in the tendency for rules to be explicitly designated by the organization, whereas routines, norms, and practices often evolve implicitly, in spoken or tacit form. A related distinction lies in traceability: while not all organizational rules are formalized (Kieser, Beck, and Tainio 2001, 600), when rules assume a written form it makes them easier to study. This is not to say that rules are more important than routines, norms, or practices because in some cases these organizational patterns are vastly more telling of the public organization's culture.

Routines are recurring patterns of organizational activity (Reynaud 2002, 69; Nelson and Winter 1982) and are also known as scripts (Ashforth and Fried 1988; Schank and Abelson 1977) and grammars of action (Pentland and Reuter 1994). A local government organization engages in a variety of routines when it opens town hall each workday at 8:00 a.m.; when it puts together a monthly newsletter for its employees; or when it begins to work on budgets every January.

Rules and routines are similar in that they both involve responses to particular stimuli (March and Simon 1958); they both conserve brainpower by creating mental shortcuts (Ashforth and Fried 1988); and they both enable efficiencies by capturing actions that have worked well in the past (Becker 2004). They also interrelate: routines can be codified into rules and rules can create routines (Nelson and Winter 1982, 106, 165; Feldman and Pentland 2003, 96).

However, there are significant differences between the two. Organizational rules generally require a higher level of intentionality and cognition than routines because routines can arise without much thinking (Ashforth and Fried 1988), whereas rules involve deliberate "if-then" statements of managerial preference for behavior(s) (Schulz 1998, 847). Routines can also exist quite separately from rules: public organizations regularly hold staff meetings, update their websites, and back up computer files without having rules dictate that they must do so. Thus, for the purpose of understanding rules in public organizations, routines are considered a distinct phenomenon.

Rules are also different from practices, or how rules, routines, and other forms of organizational preference are enacted in reality (Reynaud 2002; Nelson and Winter 1982). Practices emphasize actual behavior rather than planned or intended behavior. Sociologist Peter Blau illustrated one type of practice in his seminal work on the bureaucratic processes of two employment agencies (1963). Blau observed receptionists in one employment agency who allowed job seekers to return sooner than mandated due dates and receptionists in another employment agency who delayed job seeker returns past mandated due dates. While the receptionists may have been lower-level employees with little formal authority, their practices profoundly affected how quickly job seekers found work.

Practices derive from non-rule sources as well, including norms (Romme et al. 2011), temporal patterns (Feldman 2000, 2003), and mimetic isomorphism, that is, organizations imitating one another (Kostova and Roth 2002). This short list suggests that practices overlap with rules but are a distinct type of organizational behavior.

Norms are unwritten standards for appropriate behavior (Griffin and Moorhead 2011, 249) that impose "order without law" (Ellickson 2009). Norms lack specific triggers, like "practicing acceptable confrontation" or "working as partners together" (Denhardt, Denhardt, and Aristigueta 2012). This is not to say that norms are independent from rules. A utility billing department with a strong teamwork norm is unlikely to have rules calling for layers of signatures to approve a one-penny billing adjustment. Norms can influence the design and implementation of rules but are not rules in themselves.

So rules are distinct from routines, norms, and practices. While routines are repeated patterns of activity, practices are emergent behavior, and norms are unwritten behavioral standards, rules are explicit expectations for specific behaviors under particular circumstances. Rules are more explicit, formal, and traceable. The question to consider is whether the rules of public and private organizations are significant enough to warrant separate study.

Organizational Rules and Public Administration Theory

Public administration theory offers another lens for viewing rules in public organizations. As George Frederickson and his colleagues have observed, public administration theory spans a range of conceptual frameworks that describe, explain, or predict public administration phenomena (2012). Rules play a starring role in some theories but serve as walk-ons in others. Four public administration theories have particular relevance for organizational rules, either explicitly or implicitly: red tape, street-level bureaucracy (of the state- and citizen-agent varieties), public service motivation, and emotional labor.

The public administration theory with the most relevance for organizational rules has been identified in the red tape literature. Political scientist Herbert Kaufman wrote the first book on the subject, a slim volume that sought to reconcile the paradox of red tape as aggravating and stubbornly persistent (1977). Kaufman's explanation: red tape serves the need for compassion and social protection, both of which are public goods so valuable that we tolerate the bureaucratic hassle.

Extending Kaufman's work, public management scholar Barry Bozeman defined red tape as ineffective, burdensome written rules and he devised a theory to explain from where it comes. Bozeman cast red tape as pathology, in contrast to Kaufman, who argued for beneficial red tape (Bozeman 1993, 2000). Building on Bozeman's developmental framework, Sanjay Pandey and other public management scholars have examined differences between public and private organizations regarding red tape (Rainey, Pandey, and Bozeman 1995); they have tested the effects of red tape on managerial alienation (DeHart-Davis and Pandey 2005); they have investigated the potential for alienation to trigger red tape perceptions (Pandey and Kingsley 2000); and they have demonstrated the potential for red tape to reduce public service delivery (Scott and Pandey 2000). This rich and productive scholarship illustrates the distinctiveness of rules as a public management concern and the profound effects of rules on public employees (Bozeman and Feeney 2011).

Organizational rules also play a prominent role in both state-agent and citizen-agent theories of street-level bureaucratic behavior. Political scientist Michael

Lipsky articulated the state-agent perspective of "street-level bureaucrats," or those judges, social workers, police officers, teachers, prison guards, and public lawyers who interact with citizens (1980). From Lipsky's perspective, street-level bureaucrats are actually policymakers whose discretionary actions deviate from the spirit of the rules they are supposed to enforce. These administrators use rules and their own workloads to allocate scarce public resources. At a minimum, this rule-based rationing yields bureaucratic indifference; at worst it fosters favoritism or punishment.

The citizen-agent perspective, introduced by public administration scholars Steven Maynard-Moody and Michael Musheno (2003), provides a different take on rules. In their thinking, frontline workers view rules as both constraints to be surmounted and resources to be exploited, depending on the workers' perceptions of citizen worthiness. Frontline employees who judge citizen-clients as undeserving of public resources—because of spotty track records, lack of motivation, or unwillingness to follow instructions—will rigidly apply rules to a particular case. Frontline employees who deem citizens deserving of public resources—based on perceived redemptive qualities, empathy with a citizen's plight, or any kind of favorable impression—will apply rules creatively in the citizen's favor or work around the rules in order to reward the citizen's worthiness.

Rules play an indirect role in the theory of public service motivation (PSM), a broadly defined concept that distills to an individual's desire to serve a greater good (Scott and Pandey 2005). PSM has roots in sociology, psychology, and organizational behavior. The original definition of PSM emphasized rational, affective, and norm-based motives that public organizations are uniquely positioned to fulfill (Perry and Wise 1990). Later the definition of PSM was broadened to include an altruistic motivation to serve humankind (Rainey and Steinbauer 1999). A more recent definition mentions an individual's desire to serve a political entity that transcends individual and organizational boundaries (Vandenebeele 2007). While these definitions differ in the scope of service, they share the basic construct that PSM is a characteristic of individuals.

PSM scholars interpret the role of organizational rules in two ways. Some contend that PSM increases the likelihood that a person is "motivated by fulfilling obligations, maintaining trust, and obedience to rules" (Perry and Vandenebeele 2008, 72). These motivations encourage adherence to the "values, norms and rules that accompany government employment and conduct" (Maesschalck, Van der Wal, and Huberts 2008, 158). By extension, because PSM inculcates a respect for rules, higher PSM has been correlated with lower perceptions of red tape, presumably due to the attributions of more prosocially motivated public employees to perceive rules as legitimate (Scott and Pandey 2005). The second interpretation argues that rules (particularly bad ones) lower PSM by frustrating the goals of energized public employees (Moynihan and Pandey 2007). Combining these perspectives, PSM and organizational rules are interrelated: PSM alters attitudes toward rules and ineffective rules alter PSM.

Another public administration theory with implications for organizational rules is that of emotional labor. Emotional labor pertains to the emotive work undertaken by public employees to reconcile their own internal psychological states with organizationally sanctioned ones. While emotional labor has intellectual roots in sociology literature, Mary E. Guy, Sharon Mastracci, and Meredith Newman have firmly embedded the concept within the context of public administration. In two books and a series of journal articles these authors have found that emotional labor skills—compassion, empathy, ability to listen, stoicism—are valid empirical concepts that have gone largely unrecognized in public administration research and practice (Guy et al. 2008; Mastracci et al. 2012; Guy et al. 2010).

Public employees who practice emotional labor do so in the context of organizational rules, and their knowledge of rules informs the "hard skills" that bind the softer but equally critical emotional work. Rules affect emotional labor in two opposite ways. Rules tell employees what to do and when and how to do it, freeing up mental capacity for emotional labor. Rules also constrain emotional labor by largely ignoring it, whether in the job descriptions that structure the work, the rules that identify acceptable and unacceptable behaviors, or the policies that reward performance. Rules have the potential to alter emotional labor (Henderson 2013) but the theoretical linkages are not fully mapped.

The public administration theories here discussed focus on the interrelationships between rules and individual organization members. Public employees are shaped by rules (for better or worse) but they also use those rules to overcome the unique challenges posed by public service work. With the exception of these major streams of thought, most public administration theories are fairly silent on the role of rules in their explanatory frameworks. To cast a broader net of understanding, this book reaches beyond the confines of public administration theory to a range of disciplines in order to etch a more complete portrait of the role of rules in public organizations. The next section turns attention to the research on which the book is based.

Research Foundations

The research for this book is both original and borrowed (see the appendix for an overview). The original research comes from the Local Government Workplaces Study (LGWS), a research endeavor started in 2004 that thus far has surveyed nine very different local government organizations. LGWS studies were conducted in "cow towns," college towns, and health departments (of both the mental and physical variety). Seven organizations were located in Kansas and two were in North Carolina. Some cities were rural, others decidedly urban. The smallest employed 59 people (a small town in western Kansas); the largest exceeded 2,100 (a diverse merged city-county organization).

The Local Government Workplaces Study followed a model of engaged scholarship that combines academic research with practical managerial concerns. (There is more to come on engaged scholarship, in the final chapter.) Participating local governments sought to understand employee thinking on a range of organizational issues: workplace diversity, potential policy changes, and morale. More important, they sought low-cost (or no-cost) employee surveys. In return, the research team was granted interview and survey access to local government employees. As the principal investigator, I ensured that local government managers received an accurate reflection of employee perspectives on a range of issues important to them while collecting data that would shed light on organizational rules and generate publishable findings. Over a ten-year period the study collected interview data from 228 employees of seven local governments and 3,089 survey responses from nine local governments. Survey response rates ranged from 43 to 86 percent, with an average response rate of 53 percent.

Along with original research, this book borrows from scholars who have studied organizational rules either as the primary unit of analysis or as one dimension of a larger framework. Some of this scholarship has viewed rules in a positive light, highlighting their beneficial effects on people and organizations. This category includes scholars who view rules as containers for organizational learning (March, Schulz, and Zhou 2000); as reducers of role ambiguity (Jackson and Schuler 1985); and as facilitators of cross-organization collaboration (Vlaar, Van den Bosch, and Volberda 2006, 2007). Other scholars, such as Robert K. Merton, have expected rules to do bad things to people and their organizations, including reduce organizational effectiveness, stifle individual creativity, and render people as cogs in the machine (1940). The scholarship on red tape, a rich and productive body of work that informs the current work, does not expect negative effects from all rules but does contend that bad rules are the ones most worthy of scholarly attention because they erode precious public resources (Bozeman 2000). Some scholarship, such as the 1960s Aston Study, have viewed rules in a neutral light or as elements of organizational structure that are neither good nor bad but simply *are* (Pugh et al. 1968). Max Weber identified a mix of positive and negative effects from bureaucracy, which is unparalleled in efficiency, precision, stability, predictability, and speed (Weber, Roth, and Wittich 1978) but imposes an "iron cage" (coined by Weber's translator, Talcott Parsons) from which escape is nearly impossible (2003, 203). A different set of scholars has observed normative effects of organizational rules that depend on a range of factors, such as whether rules are enabling or coercive (Adler and Borys 1996); are experienced by employees or managers (Gouldner 1954; Blau 1963; Crozier 1964); or are designed and implemented in ways that elicit stakeholder cooperation (DeHart-Davis 2009a). These studies contribute to a fuller understanding of the role of rules in public organizations but only if we look across their contributions rather than isolate single works.

The following chapters weave this original and borrowed research together to depict a more comprehensive portrait of rules in public organizations. Original data are depicted in interview excerpts and figures are based on survey data. Borrowed research fills the contours of the portrait, spackling gaps not covered by the original research. In constructing this picture, new data is melded with existing theory to enliven a subject that serves as structural wallpaper to the public organization.

Structure of the Book

Rules occupy a unique niche in the life of public organizations. Compared with other types of organizational structures, rules level individual power rather than concentrate it. In contrast to informal routines, norms, and practices, rules shape behavior explicitly in the service of organizational objectives. Rules symbolize public values along with bureaucratic stereotypes. Rules have been vilified and lauded by management scholars but accorded only a cameo role in most public administration theory.

To provide a more comprehensive understanding of rules in public organizations, this book introduces a framework of three related perspectives: organizational, individual, and behavioral. Each perspective of the framework reports a mixture of positive and negative effects from organizational rules. The framework has a pragmatic bent and intersperses practical insights with theoretical contributions. Employing a panoramic perspective on organizational rules yields a more complete picture than can be gleaned from a single discipline or vantage point.

Chapter 1 examines rules from the perspective of the organization, that is, through the functions of rules that enable the pursuit of organizational rationality. Drawing on organization theory as well as evidence from the Local Government Workplaces Study, it tours the profound effects of the written word on the capacity of rules to shift authority from individuals to a collective, as well as the ability to disseminate organizational preferences across time and space. More discrete purposes of organizational rules are also explored: from coordinating, constraining, and empowering employees to conveying behavioral expectations and socializing employees to organizational norms and values. Rules are also examined for their capacity to create, store, and disseminate knowledge and secure legitimacy. The chapter portrays the indispensable role of rules in enabling rational action.

Chapter 2 focuses on the individual perspective, with an emphasis on how employees in public organizations experiences rules, both positively and negatively. Employees participating in the Local Government Workplaces Study reported a range of rule effects in interviews and surveys: empowerment and constraint; the legitimizing effects of rules on organizational authority; messages about procedural fairness and trust; the ability of rules to level social status; and the effects of rules on organizational identity. This chapter seeks to demonstrate that, through these experiences, rules structure the relationship between employees and their organizations.

Chapter 3 covers the behavioral perspective and examines individual responses to organizational rules. Tapping scholarship ranging from political science and economics to social work and street-level bureaucracy, the chapter examines five types of rules behavior: interpretation, compliance, violation, enforcement, and discretion. The chapter also maps influences on those behaviors. Some influences pertain to the individual: personality, gender, professional socialization, and the drive for personal power fall into this category. Other influences are organizational in nature, including performance pressures, faulty rules, and workplace culture. A third set of influences arises from interactions between the individual and the organization: legitimacy of authority, risks, the benefits of rule behavior, judgment, and peer socialization fall in this category. Rule behavior and its precursors are highly varied and complex and show that employees are active contributors to the functionality of organizational rules.

Chapter 4 applies the organizational rules framework to non-union grievance policies in North Carolina. Grievance policies were chosen for analysis because they involve a diverse set of stakeholders, including city and county managers, attorneys, human resources staff, department heads, and employees. Drawing on research into the grievance policies of North Carolina local governments, the chapter tours the historical origins of grievance policies in the United States and examines how local governments use grievance policies; how employees experience grievance policies; and how rule behaviors are triggered among managers and employees alike. The results demonstrate that the organizational rules framework enables a more comprehensive understanding of grievance policies than could be achieved by any single perspective alone.

Chapter 5 turns the organizational, individual, and behavioral perspectives into theory-based practical guidance for creating effective organizational rules. Rule effectiveness is redefined beyond purely organizational considerations to include the effects of rules on employees and the cooperative nature of rule behavior. Based on this revised notion of rule effectiveness, the chapter advises on when rules should be written, identifies attributes of effective rule design and implementation, and advocates the involvement of stakeholders in rule design. The Five-Second Rule, a doomed legal crowd control policy of the Missouri police, is used to demonstrate the consequences of not heeding that advice.

The conclusion revisits the book's major themes and identifies possibilities for the future study of rules in public organizations. Potential research topics include engaged scholarship that studies particular rules and produces management-relevant knowledge in the process; citizen-focused research that illuminates the implications of organization for democracy, social equity, and citizenship; and the potential for organizational rules research to contribute to our understanding of public policy implementation. It suggests a new way of thinking about organizational rules: as capacity rather than constraint, interaction rather than direction, and influence rather than control.

With the game plan mapped out, let us turn to the perspective of the public organization and the array of rule functions that enable rationality.

Notes

1. See the North Carolina General Assembly website at http://www.ncleg.net/gascripts /BillLookUp/BillLookUp.pl?Session=2015E2&BillID=h2&submitButton=Go.

2. See the blog of the UNC School of Government at http://canons.sog.unc.edu /the-general-assembly-preempts-local-antidiscrimination-measures/.

3. HB2 defines a person's sex as that which is stated on the birth certificate. In many states a person who has undergone a surgical sex change may have his or her birth certificate amended to reflect his or her new sex.

4. See http://canons.sog.unc.edu/the-general-assembly-preempts-local-antidiscrimination-measures/.

5. See the Gallup results at http://www.gallup.com/poll/1651/gay-lesbian-rights .aspx.

6. See the website of Channel 12 News in Phoenix, Arizona, http://www.12news .com/news/nation-now/nc-travelban-count-mounts-now-at-18-cities/134115094.

7. See the United Kingdom government website at https://www.gov.uk/foreign -travel-advice/usa/local-laws-and-customs.

8. Executive order no. G.S. 163-82.20.

9. One satire of the bill, featuring the village of Oriental, North Carolina, touts its newly hired compliance officer, Kim Daniels, who checks birth certificates and conducts

proctologic gender verification prior to bathroom admission; http://towndock.net /newsextra/bathroom-re-opens-with-on-duty-compliance-officer.

10. Declaration of President Spellings regarding Joaquin Carcano vs. Patrick McRory, US District Court for the Middle District of North Carolina.

11. It is important to note that eminent social science scholars have dismissed the distinction between public and private organizations as one of insufficient generalization (see Perry and Rainey 1988 for an overview). From these perspectives, both public and private organizations rely on resources from the environment to survive, rendering them alike at a certain level of abstraction. It is like arguing that women and men are biologically identical because at a sufficient distance their differences become blurred to the naked eye. Whether one considers public and private organizations alike or unalike depends largely on one's analytical preference.

12. George Frederickson, who has written extensively on social equity, uses the term *equity* as shorthand for the concepts of "fairness, justice and equality" (2010). His compound theory of social equity defines equity as different types of equality, e.g., opportunity, subclasses of people, rules.

13. See Schulz 2003, 1,079 for similar definitions. This definition aligns with conceptions of the organizational rule as "behaviors and requirements of jobs that are explicit" (Jablin 1987, 404); that "specifies who should do what, when, and under which conditions" (Schulz 1998, 847); and that is "legitimized by the organization" (Pugh et al. 1968, 74). The written rule is a dominant feature of Weberian bureaucracy (Adler and Borys 1996, 52; March, Schulz, and Zhou 2000, 9); it seeks a range of managerial objectives, including control, precision, efficiency, and speed (Weber 1946).

14. Unwritten rules are an important component of informal organizational structure, not to mention the precursor to written rules within oral societies (Goody 1975). While unwritten rules will be compared with written rules in the chapters ahead, they are not the focus.

15. Popular public management literature tends to conflate these concepts. To illustrate, David Osborne and Peter Plastrik conflate hierarchy and rules with their comment that "Thus government became a rule factory, with layers of managers and inspectors" (1997, 213). Similarly, David Osborne writes, "Think about the way public institutions were created during the industrial era. Typically, there was a big problem to solve; a public program was set up to solve it; bureaucracy grew; civil servants were hired to deliver services. All this was done in a very top-down, hierarchical fashion, with a great many rules and regulations" (1993, 350).

16. Max Weber, whose thinking on bureaucracy will be discussed throughout this book, died in 1920. His profound influence on social science is reflected in the many translations of his work, which is why the year of publication is so often posthumous.

CHAPTER 1

The Organizational Perspective on Rules

The organizational perspective on rules derives from a half century of organization theory. At the broadest level of abstraction, rules are the means by which organizations channel individual energy into collective goals, whether that is simply to survive (Merton 1940), manage size and complexity (Dobbin et al. 1988), reduce cognitive uncertainty (March and Simon 1958; Cohen and Bacdayan 1994; Cohen et al. 1996), imitate peers (Dimaggio and Powell 1983), or evolve into new and improved versions (Nelson and Winter 1982). More concretely, organizations use rules to achieve specific purposes (Cyert and March 1963), such as the ones that will be examined here. While these functions apply to public and private sector organizations alike, they are particularly critical for delivering public goods and services and symbolizing public values.

While this claim may seem hopelessly rational in a postbureaucratic world, it actually refers to a bounded form of organizational rationality that social scientists have recognized for many years. Nobel Prize winner Herbert Simon observed in the late 1940s that organizations strive for rationality but never quite get there. Organizational rationality is highly imperfect and far from providing the crystal clear goals, complete information, and exhaustive evaluations required to make optimal decisions (1947). Simon's version of organizational rationality is bound by the finite processing capacity of the human brain, by hazy goals with incomplete information, and by tactics that pass only minimal, not optimal, standards (79–80). From Simon's perspective, organizations pursue rather than perfect rationality, and rules are one vehicle for this pursuit.

The idea that public organizations use rules is not just theory; it is evident in the findings of the Local Government Workplaces Study. On the whole, cities and counties write rules to accomplish a variety of objectives: to control costs, protect citizens, and develop employees, to name a few. Beyond the managerial objectives that rule-writers have in mind, rules fulfill broader functions that enable goal-oriented action: coordinating, constraining, and empowering employee behavior; socializing employees to organizational values and norms; creating, storing, and disseminating knowledge; and conveying legitimacy to external stakeholders. Public organizations use rules to accomplish each of these functions, though none are accomplished perfectly.

The Written Rule and Organizational Rationality

Not all organizational rules are written, and organizations will vary in the ratio of written to unwritten rules (DeHart-Davis, Chen, and Little 2013). This variance notwithstanding, it is unwise to underestimate the power of the written rule for enabling the pursuit of rational organizational action. The advantage of having written rules is easily obscured in much contemporary public management discourse in which government is viewed as inherently inefficient and (as George Frederickson and colleagues put it in 2015), "the devil is bureaucracy" (112). Understanding the role of organizational rules in informing rational action requires a consideration of the written word itself and the ability of humans to put pen to paper.

Three aspects of organizational rationality—awareness of time, access to knowledge, and abstraction—would be difficult to achieve without the written word. Organizational rationality requires the ability to measure and track time so that the past can be understood, the future can be envisioned, and the present can be controlled. Rationality also demands abstraction, the ability to categorize people, places, and things for broader understanding and control. Rationality necessitates knowledge of goals, tactics, and potential outcomes to inform decision-making. Prior to the Greek invention of alphabetic writing in the seventh century BCE, dimensions of rationality were circumscribed by a world that communicated exclusively through the spoken word and thus lacked the means to delineate time, the ability to think abstractly on any significant scale, or the capacity to store knowledge in a permanent way (Goody 1986; Havelock 1986).

Equipped by the written word, organizational rules enable rationality by shifting authority from the individual to the organization. Max Weber made this argument in the early twentieth century when he observed that a new kind of organizational form, the bureaucracy, was "capable of attaining the highest degree of efficiency and is in this sense formally the most rational known means of carrying out imperative control over human beings" (Weber 1947, 337). It is not that Weber loved bureaucracy or believed his model to be reality versus prototype (though he has been accused of doing so; see Leivesley, Can, and Kouzmin 1994); he himself admitted that modern life creates a structure from which escape is difficult (Weber 2012, 203). Rather, Weber's point is that the legal authority that spawns bureaucracy is the only one capable of vesting power in something other than the individual.

To understand Weber's thinking on rationality, one must understand his interest in sources of authority, or "domination," as he indelicately called it (Bendix 1977, 292). Weber observed that people have legitimized authority systems in very different ways throughout history. This legitimacy enables those with power to secure the voluntary cooperation of the ruled, making their compliance something that is good and expected. Three sources of authority surfaced for Weber: charismatic, traditional, and legal-rational. With charismatic authority, the leader's personality entices people to obey based on the belief that their leader is magical and obedience will yield good things or the avoidance of bad things—think Hitler, Ghandi, or Churchill (Dow 1969). Traditional authority involves inherited power being passed down generationally through bloodlines, such as in kingdoms or the mafia (Hummel 2007, 79). This inherited power is fixed and sacred and presumably derived from divine law. Taking a current example, if Prince Charles abdicates the throne of England, the crown will pass from his mother, Queen Elizabeth, to Prince Charles's son, Prince William.

Rules and bureaucracy enter in via Weber's picture of legal-rational authority, the third source of domination. Legal-rational authority is based in the law and rules that arise out of the twin systems of capitalism and democracy. Capitalism demands efficient administration as a means of maximizing profit (Weber 1946, 223); democracy requires the leveling of the governed (226). The development of this legal authority marked a major shift in the locus of power from an individual—whether magical or predestined—to an inscribed system. As a result, Weber's bureaucracy is impersonal in comparison with the highly person-focused charismatic and traditional form of authority. This shift—from the personal to the impersonal—enables organizations to pursue collective goals that transcend the whims of the individual leader.

Weber has been criticized for being unduly optimistic about the merits of bureaucracy. The criticism is somewhat overblown: Weber simply observed the benefits of bureaucracy compared with charismatic and traditional authority systems. Consider the relative ease of establishing goal-oriented behavior in a bureaucracy versus attempting the same within a kingdom or a cult, where objectives depend on the whims of the king, the pope, or a shaman. In each of these cases organizational behavior is not driven by a collective goal but rather by the hopes, desires, and fears of a single person anointed either through his or her bloodline or by magic, not merit. Weber's take on bureaucracy can best be described as "it is what it is," which allows us to see the role of rules in rational behavior.

Evidence of the relationship between written rules and rationality is demonstrated in Figure 1.1, which compares employee responses to two questions from the Local Government Workplaces Study: *How effective is your organization in achieving the organizational mission?* and *To what extent are rules in your workplace written?* (The local government's mission statement was included with the first question.) Mission effectiveness is used here to measure organizational rationality by capturing notions of an overarching purpose being pursued by the organization with more or less success. Survey respondents indicating no written rules or few written rules in their workplaces indicate a 3.15 out of 5 for mission achievement. By contrast, survey respondents who indicate that all of their organizational rules are written give their workplaces a 3.75 out of 5 for mission achievement. This statistically significant difference lends credence to the notion that putting rules in writing increases an organization's capacity to achieve its mission.

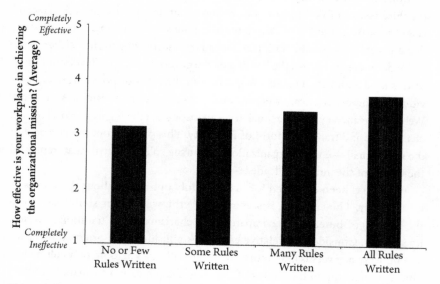

Figure 1.1 Rule Formalization and Workplace Mission Effectiveness
Source: Local Government Workplaces Study, Local Government Organizations 8 and 9, n=460.

Coordination

Organizational rules coordinate the behavior of large numbers of employees to behave consistently and cohesively on the organization's behalf (March and Simon 1958; Stinchcombe 2001; Mintzberg 1979; Blau 1974, 338; Galbraith 1977). The written quality of rules enables this coordination by providing a focal point that both guides the behavior of employees across the hierarchy and reduces conflict about how things are to be done (Becker 2004). Chung-An Chen and Hal G. Rainey provide evidence of the coordinating capacity of rules in their analysis of 2002 National Organization Survey data, in which personnel formalization (including written procedures, training, and job descriptions) correlates with teamwork among core employees. In a local government example, rules provide a template for high-dollar purchases, performance evaluations, and budget formulation, regardless of whether the department fights fires, bills residents for utilities, or transports citizens to and fro. In this sense organizational rules are like sheet music for an orchestra. One municipal fleet manager explains:

> Our departmental policies are very clear. We have safety policies, we have employee work rules, we have operational procedures and processes. To get everyone on the same page, doing everything the same way, we've had to quantify a lot of different things, to deal with workplace issues or problems, anywhere from coming to work to how we interact with people, what we do and what we don't do.

"Getting everyone on the same page," as this manager suggests, involves using rules to create shared meaning (March and Simon 1958, 184; McPhee 1985; Chen and Rainey 2013). When public employees experience an organization's rules, whether through compliance, enforcement, explanation, or discussion, they glean common understandings about both the rules' purposes, requirements, and implementation, as well as the nature of the organizations for which they work. These shared experiences enable cooperation, as explained by organizational trust scholars Katinka Bijlsma-Frankema and Rosalinde Klein Woolthuis: "Besides providing a tangible set of rules that is often used as the basis of control, codified rules and systems can provide common ground on which former strangers can develop a more abstract feeling of sharing, on which trust and cooperation can be built" (2005, 269). The shared meaning created through rules can occur across organizations as well as within them. Applying this logic to interorganizational private sector partnerships, business professor Paul Vlaar and his colleagues argue that formalization can grease the wheels of collaboration by enabling firms to make sense of and effectively cooperate with one another (2006, 2007).

Figure 1.2 provides evidence of the sheet music effect of organizational rules. Based on survey data from Organizations 8 and 9 of the LGWS, employees perceiving higher levels of written workplace rules also indicate higher levels of teamwork, a finding consistent with Chen and Rainey (2013). The effect holds regardless of whether the teamwork occurs between or within departments. Based on this evidence, written rules appear to facilitate the integration of disparate organizational parts into a cohesive whole.

Of course, organizational rules can undermine coordination, particularly when they impose contradictory requirements based on conflicting values. The

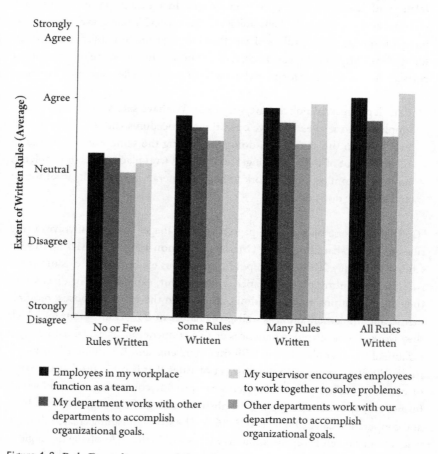

Figure 1.2 Rule Formalization and Coordination
Source: Local Government Workplaces Study, Local Government Organizations 8 and 9, n=616.

red tape literature cites this "negative sum compromise" as one precursor to the creation of ineffective or burdensome rules (Bozeman 1993, 286). Some North Carolina counties face this dilemma when they have two hiring systems, based on whether employees are covered or not by the North Carolina Human Resources Act (NCHRA). Employees covered by the NCHRA are entitled to procedural due process if they are fired, suspended, or demoted. But only county employees working in the departments of health, social services, and emergency management are covered by the NCHRA. Employees not covered by the NCHRA are at-will employees who can be fired, suspended, or demoted without procedural safeguards. Thus counties must track the personnel system under which each type of employee belongs and be prepared to impose a different system of rules with a different set of requirements and a different set of actors. The potential for conflicting personnel requirements has led some counties to consolidate and bring their own grievance procedures in line with state law, thus avoiding the potential for contradictory rules and the red tape they reap.

Constraint and Empowerment

The notion that rules only constrain is a powerful myth; in reality, organizations use rules to both constrain and empower employees. While rules can no doubt excessively constrain, and on the whole perhaps constrain more than empower, they can also impose just the right amount of control and reap a host of benefits such as social leveling, trust, and procedural fairness, to name just a few (Olsen 2006).

Rules that constrain leave little room for discretion by specifying what can and cannot by done, by whom, and under what circumstances. By contrast, rules that empower give employees latitude in the decisions they make on behalf of the organization (see Box 1.1). Scholars have focused more on rule constraint than rule empowerment (Adler and Borys 1996; Clegg 1981; March and Simon 1958, 166).[1] From the constraint perspective, rules are meant to minimize the uncertainty associated with human behavior (Merton 1940; Nelson and Winter 1982; Thompson 1961; Downs 1967). By eliminating this uncertainty, rules become "preformed decisions" (Kaufman 2006) or programs that trigger a "highly complex and organized set of responses" by specific "environmental stimuli" (March and Simon 1993, 162). Sociologist Alvin Gouldner coined this the "remote control" function of rules, allowing organizations to specify behavior across the farthest flung campus (1954, 166). Whether the rule requires letter-writers to use half-inch margins, purchasers to get five signatures, or fender-bending employees to take drug tests, rules tell employees what to do and when and how to do it.

Box 1.1 Empowerment through Rules

Here is an excerpt from an interview with a public works director that illustrates the concept of empowerment through rules.

> One policy change that I recently made delegates the authority to make adjustments to accounts. These adjustments were happening more and more and no one had a clear reason why or why not to do so. For example, there may be a billing error or we've done something causing the water bill to be high. Most of my staff wouldn't adjust the bill; they didn't want to get in trouble. Other staff members were adjusting bills liberally. But there was no paper trail and no oversight. I was getting more and more of these exceptions.
>
> I can let staff do their thing, or I can get involved personally. So I created a new staff position that handles only requests for adjustments. This person has the ability to write things off. I don't want to know about every one. And I documented this process in our policy manual. I put this change in writing as a financial sign, to create a paper trail for revenues that didn't come through.

Notice that this director crafted a rule to delegate authority for utility bill adjustments to employees in part to lighten his own workload. Prior to creation of the rule, utility bills had been adjusted inconsistently, with some employees being afraid they would "get into trouble" for making adjustments. The new rule also allowed the department to be accountable for all adjustments that were being made, which is both a public value and a tactic for demonstrating legitimacy.

Rules that empower allow discretion in individual decision-making on behalf of the organization. Discretion tends to be concentrated among professionals and higher-ups (Clegg and Dunkerley 1987) but not exclusively so: rules can explicitly allow police officers not to ticket, customer service representatives to make utility bill adjustments below a certain dollar value, or social workers to determine the levels of monitoring needed for child welfare cases. A rule can also implicitly empower through subtleties of wording: "employees should" recommends a course of action, while "employees shall" dictates it.

Like excessive constraint, too much empowerment embedded within rules can lead to dysfunction. Consider police policies that fail to identify allowable high-pursuit chases (Lum and Fachen 2008). From the LGWS, a police chief in one large Midwestern city notes:

> When I came here, there was no pursuit policy, officers could do a no-holds-barred chase, going through neighborhoods and school zones, where children will be like bowling pins. I will sit down with no more than fifteen officers and explain the rationale for the policy change. In the case of pursuit policies, I explained that the new policy would be based on the risk imposed by the chase, not the seriousness of the offense being chased. Plus, an offsite supervisor has to approve the chase. So if a supervisor hears an officer on the radio screaming about wanting to pursue a person who won't pull over, that supervisor can terminate the chase. End of story. That way it's not the adrenaline of the officer making the decision about whether to pursue or not.

The chief paints a stark portrait of the risks of having rules with too much discretion and not enough constraint. By leaving the chase decision completely to the police officer(s) involved, children can become "bowling pins" who are very much in harm's way. The absence of a pursuit policy creates unacceptable uncertainty about how and when police officers can engage in high-speed pursuits.

The idea that rules can sometimes constrain and sometimes empower may explain the contradictory results from studies on organizational rules and employee autonomy. In some of these studies employees function autonomously in the presence of written rules (Engel 1969; Child 1972); but others feel shackled by them (Pugh et al. 1968; Hrebeniak 1974). Data from Organizations 6 and 7 of the LGWS suggests that employees perceive a mix of empowering and constraining rules (Figure 1.3). Asked about the harmful versus helpful nature of their workplace rules, half of the employees indicate rules are helpful while nearly one-in-five indicate rules are harmful. One-third of employees fall in the middle, which suggests an even split between workplaces that have rules that empower and those that have rules that constrain. The next chapter will revisit the notions of constraint and empowerment when contemplating the individual perspective on rules. In the meantime, let us turn our attention to a third function of organizational rules: to convey behavioral expectations.

Behavioral Expectations

Organizational rules also convey specific expectations for individual and group behavior (Tsoukas and Validimirou 2001, 980; Kieser, Beck, and Tainio 2001,

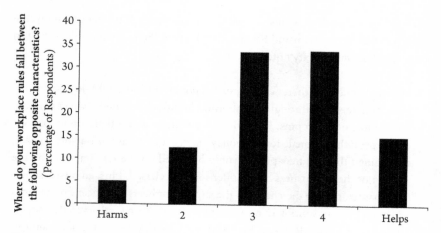

Figure 1.3 Harmful vs. Helpful Rules
Source: Local Government Workplaces Study, Organizations 6 and 7, n=872

600). Whether as simple as a no-smoking policy within city vehicles or as complex as policies on the use of social media, rules are the organizational language used to disseminate expectations across time and space (March and Simon 1958, 184). From the LGWS, one administrative assistant in a prosecutor's office provides a counterfactual:

> That's one thing that is kind of iffy in that department, because we don't really . . . I couldn't get out of a piece of paper and tell you what the rules are, because they don't really have any. That's another thing sometimes I have an issue with because some weeks you have to be there at eight o'clock; some weeks it's okay to be two minutes late, other weeks it's not. You need to have [rules] so I know what they are, and we've never really had them . . . It's not real clear-cut.

In this example the lack of rules leads to expectations that are "iffy" and not "clear-cut." The anecdote underscores the challenge of conveying behavioral expectations in the absence of rules.

To illustrate the range of behavioral expectations that can be covered by a rule, consider research by public management scholars Willow Jacobson and Shannon Tufts that examines state agency policies governing employee use of social media. The authors observe that 91 percent of on-duty conduct policies seek to protect confidential organizational information and 52 percent require disclaimers on personal websites that separate public from private personas—both of which are desirable behaviors. Regarding undesirable behaviors, 61 percent of policies preclude harassing on-duty behaviors and 78 percent prohibit conduct unbecoming a public employee, including limitations on political activity and the use of state resources for personal gain, among others. By contrast, 70 percent of these policies do not mention appropriate behavior when employees are off duty. The range of preferred behaviors embedded in these policies illustrate that organizations vary widely in the level and specificity of expectations for the conduct of individual organization members.

Figure 1.4 provides empirical support for the role of organizational rules in conveying behavioral expectations. It compares employee perceptions of role ambiguity with the extent of rules that are written. Role ambiguity is a concept of interest to organizational scholars because of its theoretical contribution to organizational morale and effectiveness. Defined as the "lack of the necessary information available to a given organizational position" (Rizzo, House, and

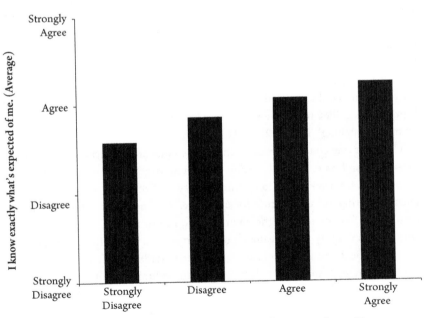

Whatever situation arises, my department has written policies and procedures to follow.

Figure 1.4 Rule Formalization and Role Clarity
Source: Local Government Workplaces Study, Organizations 1–4, n=621

Lirzman 1985), role ambiguity is a logical consequence of unclear organizational expectations. The figure—based on the perspectives of employees in Organizations 1 through 4 of the LGWS—suggests a linear relationship between rule formalization and role ambiguity: more rules in writing brings a great likelihood of knowing what the organization expects. These findings echo Jackson and Schuler's 1985 meta-analysis of nine studies with 1,300 observations, from which the authors conclude: "Formalization has the tendency to reduce role ambiguity, thus providing employees with more clarity about what is expected" (32).

Of course, behavioral preferences do not create themselves or exist in a vacuum. Rather, they are the product of values and norms held by the organization. We now turn to the socialization process that inculcates employees with values and norms and the role organizational rules play.

Socialization

Rules socialize employees to an organization's values and norms by communicating desirable and undesirable employee behaviors (Vlaar, Van den Bosch, and Volberda 2006; Ocasio 1997). Institutional scholar Johan Olsen, writing on the rediscovery of bureaucracy, argues that rules become "internalized codes of exemplary behavior, right and wrong, true and false, legal and illegal" (2006, 11). Citing Philip Jos and Mark Tompkins, Olsen notes that bureaucracies use rules "to solve the 'perennial problem of preserving character and judgment,' that is, the ability to maintain ethical reflection, give good reasons, distinguish between legitimate and illegitimate demands, and 'ensure responsible action even when no one is watching'" (Olsen 2006, 11).

Consider one county telecommuting policy that allows particular employees to work from home. The rule begins by stating its goal of reducing traffic congestion and improving environmental quality. But then the rule also prohibits telecommuting as "a substitute for childcare." By implication this rule says to employees: "We care about the environment, not so much about work-life balance. Gender equity is not really on our radar screen, nor is the working parent. The city expects your complete and undivided attention and family concerns are not to interfere." Just a few words in a rule speak volumes about an organization's norms and values.

Along with the words chosen to articulate any rule, employees are socialized by how rules are implemented. Communications scholars Erika Kirby and Kathleen Krone examine work family policies that are designed to benefit employees and the workplace discourse (by managers and coworkers alike) that discourage their use (2002). In other examples, inconsistent and unenforced rules signal that

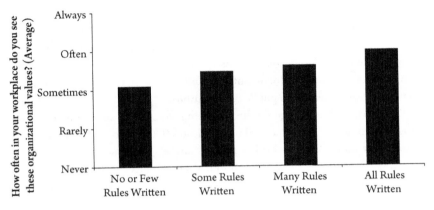

Figure 1.5 Rule Formalization and Workplace Values

the purposes for rules are superficial and unimportant. When sexual harassment policies are ignored, when emergency leave is inconsistently applied, when residency policies are upheld for some and not others—all of these lead employees to discern the sincerity of rule purposes and they are influenced to act accordingly. By contrast, consistent rule application and enforcement convey, through repetitive cues, the strength of an organization's values.

Figure 1.5 suggests the socialization effect of rules. Based on survey responses from Organization 9 employees, it depicts a comparison between employees' perception of the extent of written rules with the frequency with which employees observe specific workplace values. Employees who perceive that no rules are written also tend to observe workplace values only rarely or sometimes. When employees perceive all rules as written, they tend to observe workplace values either sometimes or often, suggesting that workplace rules make organizational values more visible than their unwritten counterparts.

By combining theory and evidence we can see the enormous capacity of rules to socialize employees to an organization's norms and values. Socialization occurs in response to the words chosen to articulate rules but also the manner in which rules are designed, implemented, and enforced. Now we turn to a different capacity of rules: creating and storing organizational knowledge.

Knowledge and Learning

Organizational rules create, store, and disseminate knowledge (March, Shulz, and Zhou 2000). While this knowledge can be conveyed explicitly (by being written down), implicitly (by being articulated but unwritten), or tacitly (by being unwritten and unarticulated), the organizational knowledge embedded in a written rule is by definition explicit.[2] Written rules are not the only form of codified knowledge—a more comprehensive short list would also include organizational charts, records, and documentation and mission statements—but they are by far the most prevalent in public organizations.

Rules codify knowledge by documenting theoretical solutions to organizational problems (March, Schulz, and Zhou 2000; Zollo and Winter 2002). Knowledge codification is both a process and an outcome of organizational learning. As a process, this codification triggers interactions between organizational members around the articulation of implicit knowledge. As Zollo and Winter note:

> By sharing their individual experiences and comparing their opinions with those of their colleagues, organization members can achieve an improved level of understanding of the causal mechanisms intervening between the actions required to execute a certain task and the performance outcomes produced. Organizational processes are often subject to significant causal ambiguity with respect to their performance implications . . . and particularly so in rapidly changing environmental contexts. Higher-level cognitive efforts and a more deliberate collective focus on the learning challenge can help to penetrate the ambiguity—although some part of it always persists. (2002, 342)

Interactions between organizational members improve the quality of knowledge by involving different perspectives on organizational issues. Kieser and Koch observed this effect in their study of two private-sector German firms, a bank and a pharmaceutical company (2008). In both settings rules were modified by an array of "internal experts" (employees who brought vastly different types of knowledge to bear on organizational problems by virtue of their experiences as potential users of the rule). Thus the bank's sales director was considered an internal expert on travel reimbursement and the pharmaceutical company's security personnel were considered internal experts on the disposal of computers no longer in use. From the perspective of employees interviewed by the researchers, the use of internal specialists to comment on rules increased both the representativeness of perspectives that should be taken into account in rule revision and the acceptability of revisions to rule users.

The writing process also produces organizational knowledge. Writing develops thought, providing it with "a coherent structure with a certain amount of orderliness, a beginning and an end" (McPhee 2004, 360). The act of putting pen to paper in and of itself is an exercise in logic, as writing is a cognitive task that renders logical propositions visible and subject to evaluation (Kallinikos 1996, 12; Flower and Hayes 1981). Indeed, the invention of the Greek alphabet was an enabling factor in the development of formal logic, as illustrated by Aristotle's *Analytics*, in which letters could be used to represent the "premises, arguments and conclusions" of a syllogism (Goody 1986, 53). Because writing enables a higher level of abstraction and yields more complex thought and scrutiny, written rules force organization members to think more deeply about cause and effect relationships (Vlaar, Van den Bosch, and Volberda 2006, 1624). As Maurizo Zollo and Sidney G. Winter note,

> Through the writing process, one is forced to expose the logical steps of one's arguments, to unearth the hidden assumptions, and to make the causal linkages explicit. Similarly, a group of individuals who are in the process of writing a manual or a set of written guidelines to improve the execution of a complex task (think of the development of a new product, or the management of the postacquisition integration process) will most likely reach a significantly higher degree of understanding of what makes a certain process succeed or fail, compared to simply telling "war stories" or discussing it in a debriefing session. (2002)

Writing benefits knowledge codification at both the individual and organizational levels. At the individual level, organizational writers are required by the inscription process to examine their own assumptions and explicate their understanding of causal linkages (Vlaar, Van den Bosch, and Volberda 2006; McPhee 2004, 358). Groups of individuals that interact around draft organizational writing, on the other hand, can acquire an awareness of broader perspectives with regard to knowledge implications and impacts (Kieser and Koch 2008).

Rule-writing produces information that is less biased and error prone and is more complete and consistent than can be produced by unwritten rules (DeHart-Davis, Chen, and Little 2013). A superintendent of a water department interviewed in the LGWS illustrates the argument:

> I don't sit in my office and think up policies by myself unless I have to. I have an internal management team, my information specialist up front, business operations manager, and my three shop supervisors. Even though there are certain things that are confidential that I can't share with them, 90 percent of the problems and issues that are brought to my desk from people in the organization, customers, or people downtown, are approached in a collective

manner. At a staff meeting, we problem-solve together. We try to carry that down to the lowest positions in the organizations. I found out a long time ago, some of your best ideas can come from those you least expect it.

This supervisor uses rule-writing as a group problem-solving exercise to involve employees from different hierarchical levels. His approach jibes with the notion of rule formalization as a type of organizational learning that enables problems to be analyzed more completely and consistently.

In addition to codifying knowledge, rules enable knowledge to be stored, retrieved, and disseminated across an organization and over time (Levitt and March 1988; Kieser, Beck, and Tainio 2001). From this perspective, a rule becomes a form of organizational memory that allows organizations to easily locate solutions to recurring problems (March and Simon 1993; Winter 1987; Sutcliffe and McNamara 2001). By virtue of their codified status, these solutions have a taken-for-granted quality that precludes the need for organizational members to look behind any abstraction or question any premise (Stinchcombe 2001, 10). The heavy cognitive lifting has been done and is stored for permanent retrieval. Consequently, organizational rules create efficiencies by reducing the need for individual members to search for solutions to recurring problems (Grimaldi and Torrisi 2001; Kieser and Koch 2008). This is not to suggest that a rule halts learning by representing the final resting point for the knowledge it embeds; on the contrary, rules perpetuate learning by making organizational processes visible (Adler 2012, 254) and by enabling their continued improvement (Nelson and Winter 1982; Adler 1993, 169; Adler 1999, 40; March and Olsen 1995, 51).

Even with all those benefits, the knowledge capacity of rules is nevertheless imperfect. Rules can induce competency traps and preclude searches for better alternatives (Levitt and March 1988); they can lead to mindless behavior and inhibit thoughtful deliberate action (Ashforth and Fried 1988); they can cause de-skilling and strip workers of competencies (Leidner 1993); and they can germinate structural inertia and slow down organizational learning (Hannan and Freeman 1984). The theoretical underpinnings of rules are also not foolproof. All rules contain predictions of human behavior, a kind of "if x then y" logic (Bozeman 2000, 87) that makes them ripe for faulty human thinking, including global and dichotomized thinking, cognitive nearsightedness, and oversimplified notions of causation (Katz and Kahn 1978, 508). When rule predictions are off the mark, they can yield "behavioral surprises" that are inconsistent with rule expectations (March and Olsen 2004, 13). This is particularly true if rules are designed without the input of organization members who can flag faulty logic

(Kieser and Koch 2008; Adler and Borys 1996). Consequently, the knowledge embedded in an organization's rules can be more or less valid and lead to rules that are more or less effective (Bozeman 2000, 157).

The potential for faulty rules notwithstanding, work by James March, James Schulz, and Xueguang Zhou provide evidence that rules are a key outcome of organizational learning. Examining the evolution of a century of rules at Stanford University, the scholars observe that rules are created at decreasing, not increasing rates (2000). They conclude: "As organizations learn how to deal with their problems, they add rules to standard operating procedures and, in effect, subtract items from the list of potential problems. As long as the supply of potential problems is fixed, each rule reduces the problem space available for subsequent rules and thus slows the rate of rule birth until something happens to replenish the problem supply." While the authors may be making heroic assumptions about the usefulness of solutions embedded in rules, or be overgeneralizing from a highly successful organization, this pattern is certainly compelling and consistent with the notion that organizational rules represent both learning and knowledge.

Legitimacy

Rules also enable public organizations to demonstrate legitimacy, defined as the extent to which an organization is acceptable to the outside world and deserving of its resources (Deephouse and Suchman 2008). "Legitimacy" is a squishy concept with a razor-sharp reality: without legitimacy, politicians slash budgets, public opinion nosedives, media scrutinize, and the regulated revolt. Under these circumstances, legitimacy is a resource for securing organizational survival (Stryker 2000).

Rules (particularly written ones) contribute to the legitimacy of public organizations, first and foremost by demonstrating compliance with the law (Weber 1947, 130–31; Rubin 2009; Sitkin and Bies 1993). For example, rules can be used to monitor water quality, track the race and ethnicity of newly hired employees, or punish acts of sexual harassment. Rules can also convey legitimacy by demonstrating best professional practices (Powell and Dimaggio 1991), such as vehicle pursuit rules based on the model policy of the International Association of Chiefs of Police. Finally, written rules demonstrate competency and trustworthiness, greasing the wheels of interorganizational partnerships (Vlaar, Van den Bosch, and Volberda 2006; 2007) that are increasingly common in public management (McGuire and Sylvia 2010). All told, rules signal that a public organization is aligned with the times and conforms to societal norms (Meyer and Rowan 1977).

Legitimacy is particularly important for public organizations, in which performance outcomes are difficult to demonstrate (Lan and Rainey 1992; Head and Alford 2008). Consider the county agency that seeks to improve the mental health of its residents. As opposed to undertaking extensive research in order to measure the elusive concept of mental health, the agency can cite with relative ease the procedures that signal it "labors on the side of the angels" (Suchman 1995, 588): its processes for quality management, its demonstrations of regulatory compliance, and its rules for patient confidentiality. This "procedural legitimacy" allows the organization to cite the rules and policies that in effect substitute for evidence that outcomes are being achieved (1995).

Of course, rules can also contribute legitimacy without imposing real operational change. This "ceremonial structure" is not necessarily harmful because it allows public organizations to respond to important audiences in ways that enable survival. John Meyer and Brian Rowan illustrate this premise in education settings, where teachers must be certified, state curricula must be adopted, and attendance must be taken—all of which leave the fundamental task of teaching unaltered (1977). However, when a rule secures legitimacy but fails to deliver social good, it can be considered dysfunctional, if not from an organizational perspective then certainly from a societal one. Thus, when federal regulators issue mining regulations but fail to enforce them, safety issues go undetected, mines explode, and miners die (Lewis-Beck and Alford 1980).

The quest for legitimacy can also prove dysfunctional when organizations become legalistic. Management scholars Sim Sitkin and Robert Bies note that organizations can mimic the lawlike practices of due process to secure the legitimacy symbolized by the legal practices themselves (1993). On the upside, legalistic organizations can empower disenfranchised workers and stimulate managerial responsiveness. On the downside, legalism can create adversarial workplaces, obscure common sense, and emphasize the letter of the law but not its spirit. Legalism can also increase the likelihood of "mock" rules (Gouldner 1954) that are on the books for appearances' sake but are unenforced in practice, susceptible to lawsuits, and undercut the very legitimacy initially sought by the rule. Ceremonial structure and legalism aside, rules are indispensable to the public organization for securing legitimacy, signaling conformity with societal norms, and thus indicating its worthiness of continued resources and survival.

Summary

The capacity of rules to serve organizational rationality depends on the power of the written word to abstract across time and space, to order time, and to accumulate knowledge. Beyond the technology of the written word, rules rationalize organizations by shifting authority from the individual to the group and enabling the pursuit of collective goals. This is not to claim that organizations are perfectly rational; only that they strive for organizational rationality (Simon 1947), in part through the use of rules. No other form of structure—not centralization, nor hierarchy, nor specialization—comes close to accomplishing the sheer range of purposes fulfilled by the organization rule.

Within the broad pursuit of rationality, rules enable discrete functions. Rules coordinate, constrain, and empower individuals in the service of organizational goals. Rules socialize employees to norms, inscribing right and wrong for all to see and conveying values held more (or less) dearly by the organization. Rules enable and produce organizational knowledge and allow problem-solving to be stored and disseminated. Rules infuse organizations with legitimacy and allow them to demonstrate their worthiness to an array of stakeholders, whether political bodies, the general public, media outlets, or regulated entities.

This is not to say that all rules function well. Conflicting rules can undermine coordination, flawed knowledge can be codified, and hypocritical organizations can use rules to gain undeserving legitimacy. Rules also can excessively constrain and convey negative messages. But without the functional aspects of rules, public organizations could not serve the social purposes for which they were designed.

Notes

1. The tendency of scholars to emphasize rule constraints rather than rule empowerment may be due to the scholarly personality, which tends to dislike authoritative controls of any kind. It may also arise from a scholarly fear of appearing overly normative rather than scientific. For commentary on this tension, see Nesbit et al., 2011.

2. See Polyani 1962, 1967.

CHAPTER 2

The Individual Perspective on Rules

If the organizational rule perspective can be summed up as *function*, the individual rule perspective is aptly labeled *experience*. Employees experience the public organization through its rules. Managers and frontline workers alike witness how rules are designed, communicated, and implemented. The consistency of rule application is compared and the consequences of rule-following and rule-breaking is observed. Employees discern positive and negative messages sent by an organization's rules, from "we trust our employees" to "employees are equally subject to the rule but some employees are more equal than others." Some employees are active participants in rule creation; others are benchwarmers or nosebleed ticket holders.

This chapter explores the nature of the individual experience of an organization's rules. Rules structure the relationship between the individual and the organization. Employees up and down the hierarchy are both empowered and constrained by rules. Rules foster the legitimacy of authority and signal procedural fairness and trust. Rules level organizational status and can shut out unjust sources of personal power. Finally, rules can forge individual identity within an organization. We will explore all of these effects and how they surface in the sociology and social psychology literatures as well as in the findings from the Local Government Workplaces Study.

Empowerment and Constraint

Students of organizational structure generally focus on how rules suck the motivational lifeblood out of employees. The argument goes something like this: Rules constrain employees and, in the process, lower morale by stifling individual creativity, undercutting employee autonomy, and creating red tape.[1]

Given their reputation as morale-killers, it is surprising to observe local government employees expressing a desire and appreciation for rules. By way of background, I began the Local Government Workplaces Study firmly expecting to get endless tape recordings of employee complaints about red tape and excessive control. But employees rarely used the term red tape. In fact, many local government employees expressed downright affection for the personnel manual, a compilation of human resource rules that spell out employee rights and responsibilities. This rules document seemed enormously important to local government employees for what can best be categorized as the *empowerment effect* of organizational rules.

Rules empower employees, first and foremost, by protecting against arbitrary and capricious action by organizational superiors. To illustrate: when a sick leave policy is in place, it becomes harder for a supervisor to allocate five days to one employee and three days to another. Sociologist Robert K. Merton recognized this in 1940: building on Max Weber's work, Merton noted that rules constrain the actions of both employees and supervisors and, in doing so, restrain the "quick passage of impulse into action" (560). Rules empower employees by protecting them from whimsical managerial behavior.

Rules also empower employees by reducing the need for supervisory permission. Sociologist Charles Perrow illustrates this type of empowerment in his book *Complex Organizations.* Perrow tells the story of Jones and his boss. The boss tells Jones there are no written rules. Jones exercises his discretion then his boss chastises him for not following protocol. As a result, Jones becomes dependent on his boss for permission to act. Had written rules been in place, Jones would not need such verbal approval and would have had freedom to act within its parameters.

Sociologist Michel Crozier observes a similar phenomenon in his book *The Bureaucratic Phenomenon,* originally published in 1965. In Crozier's study, French government workers use rules to be free of personal dependency and interaction with superiors. He notes that rules provide a countervailing force to hierarchy, which creates interpersonal dependency:

> Our final argument relies . . . on the widespread reluctance of all members of the organization to accept situations where they must depend on and be controlled by the conventional hierarchy. Rules and routines, in that sense, may have a protective value. They insure that no one can interfere in the internal affairs of the immediately inferior category. They give, therefore, a certain kind of independence. (2009, 54)

Crozier goes on to explain that a French employee's desire for independence is deeply rooted in French culture, which distrusts authority and privileges social egalitarianism. While French bureaucracy is not necessarily a model of organizational health and French culture not necessarily generalizable to a US setting, the example still lends credence to the notion that rules can be used to empower public employees by giving them freedom within boundaries.

Of course, organizational rules can constrain as well as empower, a point made by sociologists Paul Adler and Bryan Borys in a highly cited 1996 article in *Administrative Science Quarterly.* Adler and Borys argue that formalization of the work environment (whether by rules, procedures, or instructions) can treat rule followers either as problem solvers or as problems to be solved. *Enabling rules* facilitate employee problem-solving in a variety of contexts, whereas *constraining rules* impose top-down solutions that may or may not fit the situation. To illustrate the difference, consider the following two excerpts, which address funeral leave for employees from different North Carolina local government bodies:

Funeral Leave Policy #1: The City of [Everytown,] USA, understands the deep impact that death can have on an individual or a family. Therefore an employee, after completing the probationary period, may have up to three (3) days leave at full pay without charge to annual leave or sick leave when attending the funeral of an immediate family member. An immediate family member is defined as a spouse, parent, grandparent, child (or stepchild), grandchild, sibling, stepbrother, stepsister, stepparent or spouse's parents. Additional time to settle affairs of the family may be taken with the approval of the department head and should be charged to vacation leave. Leave to attend funerals of [those] other than the immediate family may be granted by the department head and charged to sick leave.

Funeral Leave Policy #2: Sick leave with pay is not a right that an employee can demand, but a privilege granted by the County of [Everyone] Board of Commissioners. Sick leave may be taken in fifteen (15) minute increments. An employee may be granted sick leave if the absence is due to . . . death in the employee's immediate family, not to exceed three (3) days, for any one occurrence. Additional leave time, under exceptional circumstances, up to ten (10) days may be authorized by the Department Head. Immediate family is defined as wife, husband, mother, father, brother, sister, children, grandparents, grandchildren, plus the various combinations of half, step, in-law, and adopted relationships that can be derived from those named. Notification of the desire to take sick leave should be submitted to the employee's supervisor prior to the leave, or not later than one (1) hour after the beginning of a scheduled workday. Such notice shall include the nature of the absence and the expected duration.

The disparity between these two funeral leave policies speaks volumes to how rules can vary in empowerment versus constraint.[2] Beyond the different level of employee benefits granted to attend funerals (three days of paid leave versus the requirement that sick leave be used), the policies use dramatically different language that illustrates the empowerment-constraint continuum. The first policy emphasizes possibility and what is allowable; the second policy focuses on confinement and what cannot take place (mentioned three times). The first policy uses positive language; the second policy uses negative language. (Note to public organization rule-writers: emphasizing that sick leave with pay is not a right is not a great way to motivate employees, period.) Department heads are able to grant funeral leave requests under both policies, but the second policy is more specific: notification must be made prior to the leave and not later than one hour prior to the beginning of the scheduled workday. The second policy views employees as problems to be solved, while the first policy gives employees a means for workplace problem-solving.

The potential for rules to either constrain or empower may explain contradictory empirical studies of the relationship between bureaucracy and employee autonomy. Some studies find that employees have more freedom in the presence of written rules; others find employee actions are shackled in their presence. Whether a rule constrains or empowers depends a great deal on how the rules is designed and implemented (a point examined in chapter 5, effective rule design). Supervisors can interpret flexible rules rigidly, rules can be designed to impose more control than necessary for achieving rule objectives, or the language of rules can be so negative that it discourages discretion, even when situations call for it.

Some evidence from the Local Government Workplaces Study suggests that written rules in general are more empowering than constraining. Consider the thrust of Figure 2.1, which compares survey participants' levels of agreement with the statement "I have the authority needed to do my job well" in relation to the extent of written rules. If organizational rules reduce employee freedom, then one would expect to see a high level of written rules associated with lower levels of perceived authority. On the contrary, the result suggests that survey respondents in workplaces with more written rules are *more* likely to feel adequately authorized. At a minimum, this result contradicts the stereotype that rules equal unilateral employee control.

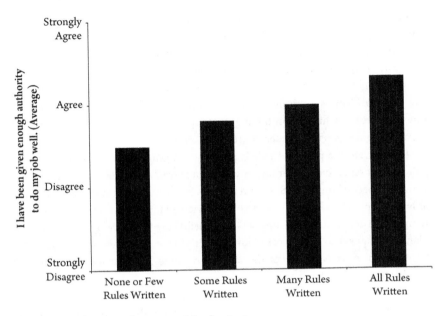

Figure 2.1 Rule Formalization and Authorization
Source: Local Government Workplaces Study, Organizations 8–9, n=622

Legitimacy

Public employees can experience rules as a source of legitimate organizational authority. Legitimacy is the perception that authority—of people, events, or structures—is "appropriate, proper, and just" (Tyler 2006). When power or authority is perceived as legitimate, people more readily accept decisions and feel obligated to cooperate (French and Raven 1959; Tyler and Lind 1992). Legitimacy of authority is thus a precursor to the acceptance of authoritative decisions and voluntary cooperation with those decisions. Legitimacy makes a public manager's life easier by getting employees to voluntarily cooperate rather than having to expend the time and energy to coerce compliance out of them. From the LGWS, one Midwestern sheriff explains: "I can make up policies all day long, but unless I can convince the deputies to follow them, I've accomplished nothing."

Written rules convey legitimacy through a "down from the mountain" quality (for an overview see DeHart-Davis, Chen, and Little 2013). The printed word looks final, official, and authoritative. This appearance of legitimacy reaps a tremendous psychological harvest: organizational policies look rational and made without regard for friendships, social status, or personal power.[3] As a point of contrast, unwritten rules do just the opposite: because they are communicated verbally they tend to derive from individual authority sources rather than from the organization as a whole.[4] The appearance of neutrality dissipates with unwritten rules, which often highlights the power of particular organizational members and raises the specter of arbitrary and capricious power.

To illustrate the power of rule legitimacy (or, rather, rule illegitimacy), consider the perspective of Tommy, a wastewater treatment plant operator interviewed as part of the LGWS. A bald and stocky thirty-something who is noticeably unhappy when he sits down to be interviewed (so much so that a vein in his temple is visibly pulsing), Tommy is responsible for the daily operations of the plant and supervises employees below him. His biggest gripe with the wastewater treatment plant is its "policy of the week" syndrome. In particular, he complains that his department head

> puts in place informal rules and things are changing all the time. Other departments don't have these policies. It creates chaos and confusion. One example is, he imposed a new rule saying if you have over nine incidences of sick leave over two hours in six months, you can be demoted, suspended, or fired. That's not a city policy and it's not right! The city's policy, I believe, is to look at patterns over time. Sick leave is either a benefit or it is not. The city is one entity, not individual islands. The rules should be signed off by human resources and two weeks notice should be given before they take effect. In another incident, the department head announced no more overtime was to be paid to plant workers, that it would be only straight time. I knew the rule was illegal and called a lawyer about it. He confirmed that the rule violates state labor law. Once I mentioned this to my supervisor, the informal rule went away.

From Tommy's perspective the department head's unwritten rules are illegitimate—"not right"—because they are not written, vetted, or sanctioned by the organization nor are they compliant with higher-order labor law. The result is "chaos and confusion" that weakens the cohesiveness of the city organization and creates "individual islands." Tommy's reaction to these unwritten rules is visceral: he is angry and willing to take action, contacting an outside lawyer to question their legitimacy.

Of course, written rules can be more or less legitimate. Red tape theory identifies illegitimate rules as those designed to serve individual self-interest rather than organizational goals (Bozeman and Feeney 2011, 56). "Green tape" theory poses a range of rule characteristics that can strengthen or weaken legitimacy, including the extent to which rules are available in writing and consistently applied (DeHart-Davis 2009a). Even when these characteristics vary, public employees generally experience organizational rules as a sign of legitimate authority, with higher compliance as the end result (DeHart-Davis, Chen, and Little 2013). The next section considers the related concept of procedural fairness, which factors into the legitimacy of all kinds of authority.

Procedural Fairness

Employees can also experience rules as a form of procedural fairness, or the extent of justice perceived in organizational processes and procedures. The idea of procedural fairness surfaced in the scholarly literature in the 1970s from research into legal proceedings (Thibaut and Walker 1975) and university grant allocation procedures (Leventhal 1980). Scholars identified two models of procedural fairness with implications for rules: the input that people have into decisions that affect them and the characteristics of the processes that make those decisions.

In 1975 social psychologist John Thibaut and law professor Laurens Walker argued that court hearing participants were more willing to accept outcomes— even disadvantageous ones—when they had the opportunity to present evidence. This input made participants feel as though they had some influence over decision outcomes, which seemed fairer, or procedurally just, to them. Building on the notion of procedural justice, social psychologist Robert Folger focused on the importance of *voice* (1977), and collaborated with Jerald Greenberg to expand the concept to organizational settings (1983).

One way that voice plays out in an organization's rules is through the opportunity for employees to weigh in on rule design. Employee involvement in rule design varies dramatically across local governments. Some local government managers see rule design as a solo exercise, while others actively and formally solicit employee feedback through committees and advisory boards. Figure 2.2 depicts the effects of voice: the more employees are involved in the design of workplace rules, the more likely they are to perceive those rules as effective. This finding is consistent with Adler and Borys's argument that employee voice is a key ingredient for enabling organization formalization (1996).

Along with voice, characteristics of decision processes (including rules) also convey procedural fairness. Social psychologist Gerald Leventhal discovered this when he observed university grant-making processes in the 1970s: six process

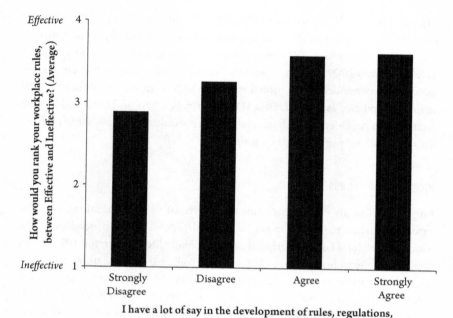

Figure 2.2   Employee Input and Perceived Rule Effectiveness
Source: Local Government Workplaces Study, Organizations 1–4, n=626

characteristics influenced whether faculty thought grant outcomes were fair or not. These characteristics included the consistency of the process over people and time; the suppression of bias (that is, no self-interested parties making decisions); the accuracy of information on which decisions were based; the correctability of bad decisions; the representation of diverse perspectives during decision-making; and the perceived fit between the ethical values of the faculty member and the ethicality that was perceived in the procedures themselves.

Of these six characteristics of fair procedures, consistency was near and dear to the hearts of the employees interviewed for the Local Government Workplaces Study. Employees across the hierarchy were keenly aware when specific employees, departments, or citizens were exempted from the rules. One 911 dispatch operator observes:

Our department's procedures are unevenly enforced. For example, during slow times we are supposed to check warrants. Some do, others don't. Some who don't are written up, others who don't are not. It could be nepotism— one guy's father is a city official—or it could be that there are only three guys versus eight women in our unit. Of one of these guys who gets away with not following the rules, people just say, "Well, that's just how he is, he's been here for a long time."

The 911 operator illustrates how employees interpret inconsistent rule application. Local government employees tend to look for sources of status to explain why the rules apply to them and not to others—in this case it's understood as family connections, gender, and seniority.

Group identity theory explains why rule consistency is so important to employees. Employees use perceptions of procedural fairness—including rule consistency—to interpret their own status, identity, and belonging within the organization (De Cremer and Tyler 2005) as well as their long-term organizational prospects (Tyler 1989). Unfair procedures lead organization members to perceive themselves as having less standing and lower group value (Bryant et al. 2010) and a more uncertain long-term relationship with their organization (DeCremer and Tyler 2005). In the context of organizational rules, employees interpret inconsistency as a signal of a lack of relative standing and worth within the organization.

Table 2.1 shows how rule consistency stacks up against employee input into making rules fair. Both consistency and employee input correlate with

Table 2.1 Employee Voice, Rule Consistency, and Rule Fairness

	Extent of Rules That Are Unfair	Extent of Rules That Are Consistently Applied	"I have a lot of say in the development of rules that affect my job."
Extent of Rules That Are Unfair			
Pearson Correlation	1	−0.39	−0.25
Sig. (2-tailed)	0	0	0
n	614	610	607
Extent of Rules That Are Consistently Applied			
Pearson Correlation	−0.39	1	.21*
Sig. (2-tailed)	0	0	0
n	610	627	617
"I have a lot of say in the development of rules that affect my job."			
Pearson Correlation	−0.25	.21*	1
Sig. (2-tailed)	0	0	0
n	607	617	627

*Correlation is significant at the 0.01 level (2-tailed).
Source: Local Government Workplaces Study, Organizations 8–9

perceptions of rule fairness, but rule consistency has a more pronounced effect. This pattern jibes with comments made during interviews: employees were generally less interested in providing input into rule design and more perturbed by rule inconsistency. Thus both stakeholder input into rules and consistent rule application are key ingredients of perceived rule fairness, but in magnitude consistency outweighs input.

Status-Leveling

Rules can be a great equalizer within organizations because they subject all members to the same requirements regardless of social status or hierarchical position. Weber identified status-leveling in his observations on bureaucracy, which for the first time in history required obedience to rules rather than to priests, kings, shamans, and mafiosi (Bendix 1977, 437). Status-leveling is illustrated by the older white male police chief who undergoes the same travel reimbursement process as the younger Latina utility billing specialist. These employees are functionally equivalent within the rule's domain, regardless of the fact that they reside within vastly different organizational and social realities.

Written rules are able to level status differences between people by virtue of the written word. Writing yields a "different kind of relationship between the word and its referent, a relationship that is more general and more abstract, and less closely connected with the particularities of person, place and time, than obtains in oral communication" (Goody and Watt 1963, 321). In service of status-leveling, writing enables people, places, and things to be categorized and thus more easily assigned equal rights and obligations. (It is no coincidence that the invention of alphabetic writing preceded the creation of democratic systems of taxation and census-taking.) Speech, by comparison, tends to be tailored to the audience at hand, which makes it less adept at abstraction and more susceptible to status-based manipulation of content. The adaptability of speech makes unwritten rules well suited to context-dependent directives but less so at ensuring equal treatment of public organization members during rule implementation.

To see how unwritten rules raise questions of bias and individual standing, consider this quote from a female scientist in a 2011 study by Wendy Roth and Gerhard Sonnert of an "anti-bureaucratic" research organization:

[I] very much . . . believe that things like gender equity rely on having policies that are open and clear and are being implemented the way people expect them to be. And then it's this loosey-goosey kind of, you know, there aren't any rules because we'd rather make deals because that way we can make more people happy. It leaves out the people who didn't know you were supposed to be making a deal. And that tends to be the women and the minorities and the less-aggressive men. And it isn't because it's . . . gender discrimination, but it leads to it. (12)

The scientist perceives unwritten rules as favoring those who know how to "make a deal," in this case forceful white men. She does not perceive the discrimination as direct but rather as an indirect consequence of unwritten rules that create an unlevel playing field.

Recent public administration research provides supporting evidence that rules level the organizational playing field. In a study of city administrators and police officers, Shannon Portillo finds that women, minorities, and younger people use rules to legitimize their own authority, particular in enforcement situations where they have less societal status (2012). Three additional analyses are based on Local Government Workplaces Study data. In analyzing Organization 6 data, public management scholar Randall Davis finds that employees committed to unions perceive less organizational red tape (2012). He explains that, because unions exist to level power differences between management and workers, and rules level the organizational playing field, it follows that employees with greater affinity for unions perceive less red tape. (Davis also finds that interacting with other union members increases red tape perceptions.) Two additional analyses of the Local Government Workplace Study relate to gender and rule perceptions: female public employees generally perceive organizational rules more favorably than their male counterparts (DeHart-Davis 2009b) and report more positive attitudes toward rule abidance (Portillo and DeHart-Davis 2009). A final analysis by Christine Rush and Edward Kellough found that female respondents to a survey of county administrators and department heads had a more accurate understanding of equal employment opportunity law than their male counterparts (2015). Results from these studies reveal that rules are observed, understood, and used differently by organizational members with lower societal status and suggest that rules level social status within public organizations.

Status-leveling from rules is not limited to the public sector: research on private firms suggests that for women and minorities, written rules lead to higher pay, more executive positions, and greater professional resources. Written human resource rules have been correlated with higher proportions of women in core scientific roles within high-tech startup firms (Baron et al. 2007); higher representation of women, minorities, and disabled persons in both managerial and nonmanagerial positions (Leek, Saunders, and St. Onge 1992); lower percentages of male managers (Reskin and McBrier 2000); and higher earnings for women, more so than men (Anderson and Tomaskovic-Devey 1995; Elvira and Graham 2002). Evidence of the role of bureaucratic structure is found in the higher percentages of women employed by private contractors to the federal government (Linnehan and Konrad 1999) as well as the number of women employed at the executive levels of more structured engineering and aerospace firms (Cook and Waters 1998; McIlwee and Robinson 1992).

On the flip side of the equation, unwritten rules have been noted for their potential to encourage "cronyism, subjectivity, sex stereotyping and bias" (Reskin and McBrier 2000) and to obscure promotion criteria and introduce gender-biased performance evaluations (Roth and Sonnert 2011; McGuire 2002; Baron et al. 2007). Unwritten rules and other forms of "structurelessness" have also been noted for concentrating unaccountable power in the hands of a few (Freeman 1972). In related supporting evidence, public administration scholars Jeffrey Wenger and Vicky Wilkins have found that for female claimants, automated telephone unemployment insurance claim processes produced more favorable results than in-person claim processes, with no differences detected for male claimants (2009). Put another way, women filing for unemployment insurance claims are better off phoning in their claim and not asking a human to approve it.

Though written rules enable status-leveling, they do not guarantee it. After all, written rules also can be designed to maintain or strengthen the power of dominant social groups (Bielby 2000, 123; Jewson and Mason 1986); they can be applied inconsistently based on organizational status (Gouldner 1954; Bielby 2000, 125); or they can be followed only to meet the letter but not the spirit of the law (Edelman 1992; Edelman and Petterson 1999). In the case of unemployment insurance, state agency rules can be written in ways that render low-income women ineligible for filing claims, such as a rule that says that leaving a job due to lack of childcare, domestic abuse, or sexual harassment is inadequate (Wenger and Wilkins 2009, 317).

A more recent example comes from United Parcel Service, which landed in court for refusing a pregnant employee light-duty work.[5] Attorneys for the shipping giant argued that the policy was meant to cover disabled workers, not pregnant ones. (UPS has since changed its policy to allow pregnant workers to qualify for light duty.) This specific instance supports the general contention of many feminist scholars that standard bureaucratic structure is bad for women. The ill effects include feminizing subordinates to play feminine-subservient roles (Ferguson 1984); conceptualizing workers as asexual (i.e., as only male; Acker 1990); inadequately valuing emotional labor skills (Guy and Newman 2004);

personifying masculine imagery (Stivers 2002); and privileging masculine values over feminine ones (Duerst-Lahti and Kelly 1995).

While rules can codify status privileges, the evidence suggests that rules have an even greater potential for reducing prejudicial behavior. Police officers and city managers who are women or racial minorities use rules to legitimize their authority (Portillo 2012); employees committed to unions perceive less red tape (Davis 2012); women in local government perceive rules more favorably and indicate less rule-bending than their male counterparts (DeHart-Davis 2009b; Portillo and DeHart-Davis 2009); and private firms with more layers of bureaucracy provide better career opportunities for women and minorities (Baron et al. 2007; Leek, Saunders, and St. Onge 1992; Reskin and McBrier 2000; Anderson and Tomaskovic-Devey 1995; Elvira and Graham 2002). No doubt some organizational rules can oppress women and minorities (intentionally or unintentionally), but on balance rules appear more likely to level the organizational playing field.

Trust

Organizational members also experience rules as trust or distrust. Trust is the expectation of benevolent or benign future behavior by others.[6] Uncertainty plays a role in trust because harm is always a possibility. Trust then becomes the perceived likelihood that harm is possible but improbable.

Rules convey the extent to which managers trust employees and are trustworthy themselves. Trust makes a public manager's job a thousand times easier by getting employees to behave voluntarily in ways that benefit the organization (Tyler 2003). Without trust, managers resort to coercion, specifying exactly what needs to be done, monitoring employee behavior to make sure it happens, and imposing negative consequences when it does not. Coercion is enormously time-consuming and resource-intensive and can *still* be ineffective: the secretary may deliver the message promptly, or not; the fleet maintenance operator may still sneak a smoke in the parking lot; the department head might continue to sexually harass.

The most important effect of rules on trust is to signal to employees how much management trusts or does not trust them. From the LGWS, employees perceiving burdensome rules also believe that supervisors do not trust them (Figure 2.3). This finding jibes with the notion that excessively controlling rules ask employees to "check their brains at the door" (Adler and Borys 1996, 83) and suggests a lack of faith in employees to do what needs to be done (Long 2010,

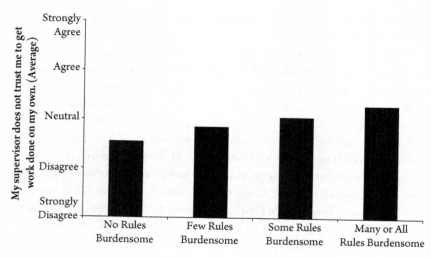

Figure 2.3 Burdensome Rules and Supervisory Trust
Source: Local Government Workplaces Study, Organizations 8–9, n=608

370). On the other hand, rules that impose the right amount of control—just enough to accomplish rule objectives—say to employees: "We assume that you have the brains and the skills and the ability to do what needs to be done without being micromanaged."

Consider this interview excerpt from a utility billing customer service representative: "We have a rule that requires me to seek authorization for adjustments to utility bills regardless of how small the amount. It's a waste of time, both mine and the customer's. Please give me a dollar amount below which I can authorize it myself." From this employee's perspective, the city is signaling that she cannot be trusted to make a one-penny adjustment to a utility bill. The city's need to control employee behavior exacts an emotional toll and makes employees believe that they are viewed as incompetent and unable to make even the smallest decisions.

Along with conveying trust in employees, rules also signal the trustworthiness of public organizations themselves and suggest that employees can count on the organization to behave benevolently in the future. Rules convey trustworthiness by making managerial behavior predictable. They signal organizational competence and require managers to behave in ways that are trustworthy. Predictability is a key ingredient because trust is built, in part, on expectations of human behavior (Sitkin 1995). Rules are made predictable by being applied consistently, that is, without giving systematic exemptions to particular people, groups, or citizens (DeHart-Davis 2009a). The late organizational behavior scholar Ellen Whitener and her colleagues explain how consistency serves trust:

> Behavioral consistency (i.e., reliability or predictability) is an important aspect of trust . . . trust reflects the willingness to be vulnerable to the actions of another party and the willingness to take risks. . . . If managers behave consistently over time and across situations, employees can better predict managers' future behavior, and their confidence in their ability to make such predictions should increase. More important, employees become willing to take risks in their work or in their relationship with their manager. Predictable, positive behavior reinforces the level of trust in the relationship. (1998, 516)

As expected, inconsistency in rule application has the opposite effect: it signals to employees that public managerial behavior is unpredictable *despite* the presence of a rule that should make it so. Inconsistency is especially damaging to trust, given a manager's willingness to ignore his or her own organization's preferences and behave unpredictably. From the LGWS, employees of Organizations 1–4 illustrate this relationship loud and clear: the more inconsistently applied rules are perceived as a problem, the less trust they feel toward upper management (see Figure 2.4).

A rule conveys trust or distrust depending on the apparent "competence" of the rule itself, a concept devised by business professors Joel Brockner and Phyllis Siegel. Rule competence is partly the appearance of a rational rule-design process: defining the problem, identifying alternative solutions, and evaluating each alternative according to fixed criteria. Having such a process in place for rule development suggests that the organization "has its act together" (Brockner and Siegel 1996, 407) and is worthy of being trusted.

A third way that rules convey trustworthiness to employees is by holding managers accountable for trustworthy behavior.[7] As Bies and Tyler note, "The creation of formalized procedural safeguards makes more salient the accountability and responsibility of managers. . . . As such, increased formalization may act to restore employee trust in managers" (1993, 362). From the LGWS, having rules in writing correlates with employees' belief that supervisors are truthful and benevolent (see Figure 2.5).

Rules that mandate ethical behavior toward employees, that require employees to be treated with respect, and that implement fair processes all suggest that the organization has benevolent intentions toward its employees. Of course,

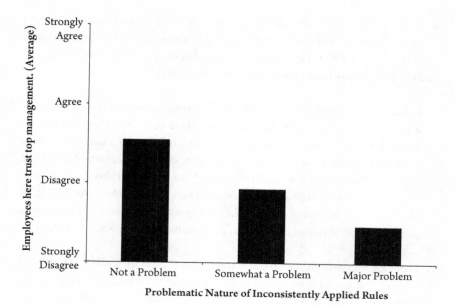

Figure 2.4 Inconsistently Applied Rules and Employee Trust
Source: Local Government Workplaces Study, Organizations 1–4, n=627

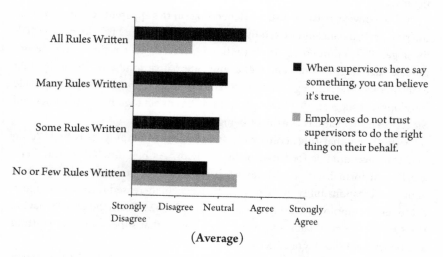

Figure 2.5 Rule Formalization and Supervisor Trustworthiness
Source: Local Government Workplaces Study, Organizations 8–9, n=616 and n=617

if those same rules are errantly interpreted or not applied at all, they signal the untrustworthiness of the organization to employees. (For an illustration, see Box 2.1.)

Organizational Identification

Public employees can also experience rules as a source of identification with their organization. This argument was first raised by organization behavior scholars Charles Greene and Dennis Organ, who wondered about the effects of bureaucracy on professional employees such as scientists and engineers. Greene initially suspected that rules would lower morale by causing professionals to feel pulled between professional and organizational norms, a phenomenon known as "role conflict." By examining survey data from private sector scientists and engineers, the findings confirmed his suspicions: survey respondents who identified more strongly with their professions than their organizations did indeed feel more alienated, an effect that was rendered more intense by rules. However, Organ and Greene's subsequent work identified a more nuanced effect: while rules may increase role conflict, they also exert a positive effect on the clarity of organizational expectations and identification and result in a net increase in morale. The scholars explain: "Formalization provides a framework for the professional to view his contributions to the organization and the organization's contributions to his professional goals" (Organ and Greene 1981, 251). Figure 2.6 supports this organizational identification argument: rule formalization is

---

Box 2.1 How One Rule Made a Local Government Look Untrustworthy

Consider a policy requiring employees to self-report when they have taken cold medicine. The policy arose out of concern that cold medications impair judgment and lead to employee safety issues. The policy was formulated in the vacuum of a few rule designers and without the input of employees or other stakeholders; it prevented the opportunity to develop a shared understanding of the issue. Employees responded to the rule by wondering, "Is the organization planning to sue me in case something happens when I've taken cold medicine?" Managers had failed to consider the signals that such a policy would send to employees, including the possibility that it would be construed as management's desire to amass evidence to be used against employees (implying nonbenevolent future behavior on behalf of the employer). The rule was designed but never implemented.

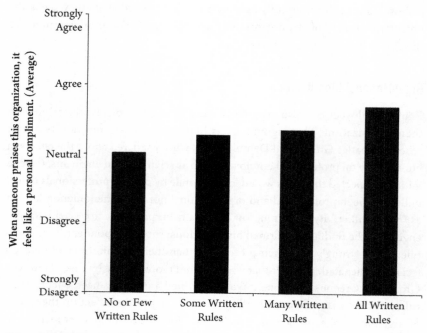

Figure 2.6 Rule Formalization and Organizational Identification
Source: Local Government Workplaces Study, Organizations 8–9, n=614

associated with greater agreement among survey participants that praise for their organizations feels like a personal compliment (survey question adapted from Mael and Ashforth 1992). Thus, written rules serve as one point of mental connection between employees and their organizations.

Summary

Looking across these effects, we see the profound influence of rules on people in public organizations. Organizational rules can mold or fracture relationships with employees. Rules empower and constrain people, render authority palatable through legitimacy, and signal that the organization is fair and just. Rules level societal status so that people from vastly different backgrounds can interact on equal footing within organizational settings. Employees glean from rules how much the organization trusts them (a lot or not at all) and how much the organization can be trusted. Rules can strengthen or weaken organizational identification by rendering visible the employee-organization relationship. Cumulatively these rule effects send powerful signals about the true nature of the public organization and the individual's relative standing and worth within it. In the next chapter, we consider the behaviors that arise within and beyond the nexus of organizational aims and individual experiences.

Notes

1. See DeHart-Davis, Davis, and Mohr 2014 for an overview of this literature.

2. To read more policies like these, search the Internet using the words "understands the deep impact that death can have on an individual or a family" or "Sick leave with pay is not a right that an employee can demand."

3. The legitimacy of the written rule is different from Barnard's "zone of indifference," which pertains to an employee's apathy regarding orders to be followed. Zones of indifference are theoretically determined by "the degree to which the inducements exceed the burdens and sacrifices which determine the individual's adhesion to the organization." One key distinction between legitimacy and zones of indifference is that the former inspires commitment while the latter leads to disinterest.

4. One could argue that common law, which arises from court decisions, entails unwritten rules that transcend particular people. However, as demonstrated in the introduction, law and organizational rules are two different units of analysis.

5. Young v. United States Parcel Service, Inc., Supreme Court of the United States, No. 12-1226 (2015).

6. For an overview and definitions of trust, see Whitener et al. 1998; Sitkin 1995; Reynaud 2002; and Brockner and Siegel 1996.

7. One point of counterevidence to keep in mind: some scholars have found that formalization lowers employee perceptions that managers are trustworthy. One such study was conducted among business students in China by scholars Li, Bai, and Xi (2012). Their measures of formalization were, however, communications, resistance to change, rule-bending, and relationships, but not written rules. As will be discussed in the final chapter, it is not uncommon to measure formalization in ways that transcend written rules and conflate concepts.

CHAPTER 3

The Behavioral Perspective on Rules

> "Rules are so routine, they are like breathing. In engineering, everything involves structure and standards. I keep the procedure manual for the office at my desk. It helps me and others to know what to do. I follow rules every day."
> —PUBLIC WORKS ADMINISTRATIVE ASSISTANT

> "When you are charging patients, you need someone very impartial. There are rules on how they are supposed to charge. But if a friend comes in, the front desk will break the rules and manipulate the data to make sure they don't pay as much."
> —PUBLIC HEALTH NURSE

> "I think the policies are interpreted differently at each level within the organization. I work in a department with four divisions, where policies are looked at a little differently, maybe a little bit more lenient in some areas and more strict in other divisions."
> —ENVIRONMENTAL SCIENTIST

Rules in public organizations trigger an array of behaviors. As illustrated by the above excerpts from the Local Government Workplace Study (LGWS), some rule behaviors are compliant, while others are rebellious; some are organizationally harmful, while others are neutral or beneficial. Like all bureaucratic behavior, rule behavior shapes the pursuit of public interest and the effectiveness of bureaucratic structure (Wise 2004). It signifies the legitimacy of authority (DeHart-Davis, Chen, and Little 2013); the effectiveness of group functioning (Tyler and Blader 2000); and the strength of public sector accountability (Romzek and Dubnick 1987).

This chapter delves into the behavioral perspective of the organizational rules framework, especially the spectrum of rule behaviors and their influences. The behavioral perspective draws on a diverse body of scholarship, from economics and political science to social work and street-level bureaucracy (SLB) research. There are shades of compliance, violation, and enforcement, along with interpretation and discretion. An array of influences on rule behavior are mapped: some that characterize the person, others that stem from the organization, and still others that arise from the confluence of both. This compilation of rule behavior is etched from organizational scholarship with support from the Local Government Workplaces Study. We begin by exploring the variegated nature of rule behavior.

Rule Behavior

It would be tempting to construe rule behavior as a dichotomous choice between following or breaking a rule. Indeed, early ideas about bureaucracy took for granted that rules would be followed because doing so showcases one's expertise and ensures upward professional mobility (Weber 2013, 196 and following; Merton 1940). Scholarly awareness of rule-breaking emerged in the 1950s, when field researchers in sociology observed that organizational rules were being violated in creative and productive ways (Gouldner 1954; Blau 1963). Since then, scholars have uncovered a divergent spectrum of rule behaviors in far-flung settings that span governments and corporations, from the reception area to the executive suite.

This literature, along with evidence from the Local Government Workplaces Study, depicts five categories of rule behavior: interpretation, compliance, violation, discretionary rule behavior, and enforcement (Figure 3.1). Rule interpretation involves divining organizational intent and assigning meaning to the situation at hand. Compliance is the most common rule behavior but it is not always organizationally beneficial: rules can be followed rigidly, maliciously, or excessively. Rules can be violated in part (rule-bending) or in toto (rule-breaking), for good or bad reasons and with prosocial, malevolent, or self-interested intent. Discretionary behaviors surface in the gray zone of an organization's rule, where public employees are authorized (either explicitly or implicitly) to make decisions about a rule's implementation. Enforcement involves all these rule behaviors, as well as the need to explain rules, monitor compliance, and administer noncompliance consequences. While not mutually exclusive or exhaustive, these categories have heuristic value for discerning the spectrum of behaviors triggered by organizational rules. Rule interpretation, the least observable rule behavior, launches the discussion.

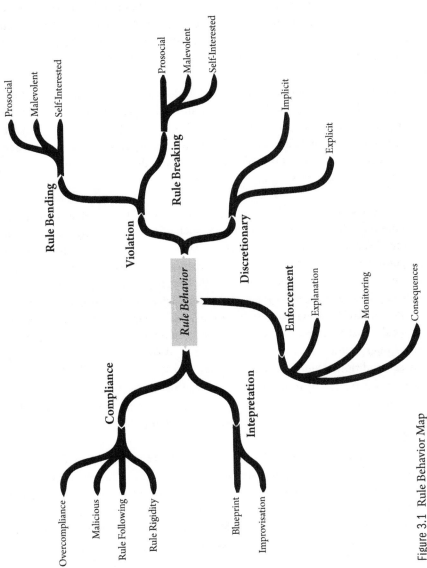

Figure 3.1 Rule Behavior Map

Interpretation

All rules are interpreted at some point and on some level. Rule interpretation translates a rule's intent and assigns its meaning to the situation at hand. In referring to one London Health Department report, social work scholars Tony Evans, Mark Hardy, and Ian Shaw call attention to the fact that "policy does not come neatly tied up in sealed packages" (2010, 108). From the Local Government Workplaces Study, a building codes inspector further elucidates:

> We have written and unwritten rules. Most codes are in black and white. When they are not, you figure them out. It takes years for unclear codes to become effective. I figure out unclear codes by compiling information on the intent of the rule. When I understand where codes come from, I am able to explain them better. This allows me to interpret them better. I do my best to understand code reasoning.

The inspector discerns several aspects of rule interpretation. First, some rules require more interpretation than others, such as those provided "in black and white." Second, knowing the organizational intent of a rule aids interpretation (a point that will be elaborated on in the chapter on effective rule design). Third, more interpretation is needed for rules that are newer and vaguely worded, as suggested by his statement, "It takes years for unclear codes to become effective."

Beyond the building inspector's insights, the red tape literature also suggests that rules that are infrequently used or that conflict with other rules will require more interpretation on the part of employees (Bozeman 1993, 2000). Flipping these conditions around, less interpretation will be required of rules that are older, more frequently used, or clearly worded and understood.

The idea of interpretation raises questions about the nature of rules. Do rules have no meaning apart from their application (Wittgenstein 2010; Evans and Hardy 2012a; Manning 1977)? Or are rules like software programs that trigger prespecified actions (March and Simon 1993, 162) and reduce the need to "look behind the abstraction" (Stinchcombe 2001, 10)? The answer to both is yes. Rules sometimes emerge as they were envisioned and sometimes depart wholesale from the original intentions. This is why rules cannot be understood as either-or propositions. Rules are design and implementation, blueprint and improvisation, and top-down and bottom-up all at once.

Compliance

Scholars give less attention to rule compliance than rule violation, perhaps because compliance is a less-intriguing topic. As one administrative assistant in a prosecutor's office explains, "I don't see many rules ... I wouldn't say that there are really good ones or bad ones, there just aren't any until you break them." Public management scholar Erin Borry interprets this comment as "particularly interesting because public organizations are so rule-laden that perhaps rules are not a consciously significant part of the job: they just simply are" (2013, 67).

To what extent are rules followed within public organizations? Empirical evidence on this question is scarce. Most street-level bureaucrats appear to behave consistently within the law and policy (Maynard-Moody and Musheno 2003, 93), while a tiny percentage of social workers fudge paperwork (Brehm and Gates 1997, 122) and paramedics appear to largely follow medical protocols (Henderson 2013).

In the LGWS, rule-following appears to be the norm. Figure 3.2 overlays the responses to two types of questions about rule compliance. The employees of Organizations 6 and 7 were asked to characterize workplace rules on a scale

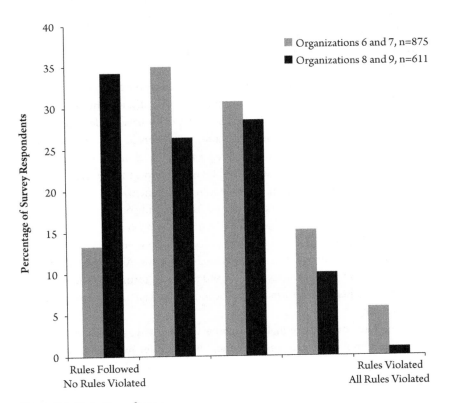

Figure 3.2 Rule Compliance
Source: Local Government Workplaces Study

between "violated" and "followed." Forty-eight percent placed their workplace rules on the followed side of the scale, 21 percent on the violated side of the scale, and nearly 31 percent somewhere in the middle. When asked about the extent of workplace rules that were violated, employees of Organizations 8 and 9 suggest that rules are largely followed: 60 percent indicate that no rules or a few are violated, while only 11 percent see many or all rules violated.

Generally speaking, rule-following can be construed as organizationally beneficial and indicative of effective public organizational leadership (Tummers and Knies 2014), legitimacy (Tyler and Blader 2005), and rule effectiveness (DeHart-Davis 2009c). But such a conclusion depends on the assumption that public managers seek to pursue social good through rational means. This assumption is not always warranted. Consider Adolph Eichmann, the Nazi lieutenant colonel who cited rule-following as an excuse for committing unspeakable evil (Osiel 2001). Or the United Nations staffers who used rule-following to justify their passive observance of the Rwandan genocide (Barnett 2002). Or the public employees who willingly follow rules that are illegitimate, burdensome, or just plain stupid (Bozeman and Feeney 2011). Rule-following can be organizationally and societally beneficial, but this is not always the case.

Even when rules serve legitimate and moral purposes, not all types of rule compliance can be categorized as positive. Rule rigidity is one such variant. Rigid rule followers reject discretion and interpret rules literally, whether suggested by the context or not. Sociologist Robert K. Merton observed rule rigidity in his seminal 1940 paper, "Bureaucratic Structure and Personality." Merton coined the terms *mid-range theory, unintended consequences,* and *self-fulfilling prophecy.* He argued that bureaucracies encourage employee behaviors that are ultimately dysfunctional for the organization. Rules require discipline, which in turn requires "devotion to duty, sense of limits of one's authority and competence, and methodological performance of routine activities." From Merton's perspective, a desire to be disciplined leads employees to construe compliance as an end rather than a means of achieving broader organizational goals. As a result, employees become rigid in their responses to rules and produce "formalism and ritualism," "punctilious adherence to formalized procedures," and an inability to deliver services to clients.

Compliance can also be malicious, otherwise known as "working to a rule." Malicious compliance leads one to adhere to the letter but not the spirit of a rule. Through malicious compliance, employees send an "I'll show you" message that conveys dissatisfaction or autonomy. Underspecified and illogically designed rules are particularly vulnerable to malicious compliance. Firefighters provide one example. Beginning in the early twentieth century, firefighters were required to wear a self-contained breathing apparatus (SCBA) to protect them from smoke. Firefighters generally disliked the apparatus because it "hampered visibility, flexibility, and maneuverability" (Gagliano, Phillips, and Jose 2008, 13). To circumvent wearing the heavy gear, firefighters would put the apparatus on their backs but not on their faces. Firefighter compliance was malicious in that it took advantage of the rule's poor specification. But it came at great cost: some firefighters died when they unexpectedly encountered smoke without the mask (233).

Over-compliance, or going above and beyond rule requirements to do more than necessary to comply, is another type of adverse compliance. Over-compliance has been detected within the regulatory arena, in university reactions to tighter federal overhead requirements (Bozeman and Anderson 2014) and responses to new air quality permitting rules by industrial firms (DeHart-Davis and Bozeman 2001). While these examples are regulatory in nature, Box 3.1 (Illustrating Over-Compliance) provides an organizational illustration. Given that public organizations face ever-tightening fiscal constraints, over-compliance is an inefficient use of precious resources.

It is fortunate that rule-following appears to be the norm, given the negative organizational consequences of other compliance variants. Rule-rigidity is maddening and ineffective; over-compliance wastes organizational resources; malicious compliance is potentially damaging to the organization and its members. We turn next to the range of behaviors associated with rule violations, each of which can trigger a unique set of positive and negative organizational effects.

Rule Violation
The violation of a rule involves deliberately deviating from rule requirements without approval, excluding noncompliance that is accidental, due to ignorance, or sanctioned by the organization (Sekerka and Zolin 2007). Within the category of rule violation, rules can be either bent or broken. Rule-bending involves a violation of only one or some parts of a rule; rule-breaking involves ignoring rules in toto. Examples of rule-benders who grace the pages of public management scholarship include employees who "fudge" paperwork to help clients (Brehm and Gates 1997; Maynard-Moody and Musheno 2003); unemployment agency receptionists who shorten mandatory minimum time frames before which jobless clients can return for reapplication (Blau 1963, 29); and project team members who split up purchase orders to expedite processing time for national defense hardware and software (Sekerka and Zolin 2007, 237). Rule-breakers are personified by Gouldner's gypsum miners who disregard corporate no-smoking policies (1954, 182); O'Leary's "Nevada Four," who usurped US

Box 3.1 Organizational Over-Compliance

One Monday morning the faculty members of a university department received an email from an administrator stating that all travel reimbursements involving personal vehicles must, henceforth, include a Google map of any mileage driven. If only one route is taken, the administrator will print the route; if two or more routes are taken, faculty members are to print the routes themselves and submit them with their travel reimbursement paperwork.

A great hue and cry arose from the faculty, with emails flying at the speed of light. The faculty labeled the new policy ridiculous Orwellian red tape. The administrator who sent the original email responded that the policy follows university orders.

Being a student of organizational rules, I emailed an acquaintance in the university's administrative apparatus to get clarification. My acquaintance also emails the department head in charge of travel reimbursements. My acquaintance and his colleague soon email back and explain that the rule has been misconstrued and that there is no such mapping requirement. True, reimbursements will be processed more quickly if mileage documentation is attached. But the university does *not* require that maps accompany personal mileage reimbursements. A sheepish email from departmental staff seeking to clarify the miscommunication soon arrives.

How did this over-compliance happen? Apparently one person in charge of explaining the rules—who was moderating a webinar on university travel policies—made the proclamation. It is unclear what the conclusion had been based on, and or why. And over-compliance can be attributed to an array of factors. Perhaps the administrator had a bureaucratic personality that tended toward stringent rule interpretation and a strict rule interpretation made him or her feel empowered. Perhaps the administrator was socialized to interpret rules rigidly. Maybe the culture of the administrator's workforce favored compliance over customer service. Perhaps the pressure to rapidly deliver information yielded a split-second (albeit inaccurate) response. Regardless of which of these explanations is valid, it is apparent that the rule behavior in question had a tangible ripple effect at the university that drained resources in the name of control.

Department of Interior irrigation practices (2013, 41); and Manning's narcotics officers who ignore purchasing rules (1977).

Rule violations can also be categorized by the actor's intent (Morrison 2006). Prosocial rule violators act only to help an organization or its stakeholders. Erin Borry's parks and recreation supervisor, who deviated from protocol to allow interns to wear shorts in 100-degree heat, falls into this category (2013, 66). Malevolent rule-bending, on the other hand, is meant to inflict damage on the organization, as identified by Vardi and Weiss as behaviors such as theft, harassment, and loafing (2004). Self-interested rule-bending is done to benefit individual employees, as did Sekerka and Zolin's Department of Defense acquisition managers (2007), who disregarded mandatory testing of network security because they wanted to leave early after a marathon work session.

Sometimes rule-violators blur categories of intent. In one example, unemployment counselors violated state law by failing to report racially biased employer hiring practices and secretly coding high school job fair attendees by race, even instructing employers on how to racially discriminate without getting caught (Cohen 1965; 1970). In using reasoning that today would be considered both illegal and immoral, the counselors professed prosocial motivations for these human rights violations: to avoid getting important community employers in trouble, to retain "discriminating" clients, and to spare the feelings and cab fares of racial minorities who would not be hired. What is considered prosocial rule-bending varies over time and by culture and societal power structure.

Which motivations dominate rule behavior? If Figure 3.3 is any indication, employees are more likely to be bent for prosocial rather than self-interested reasons, a result consistent with the conclusions drawn by organizational behavior researchers (Blau 1963; March 1994, 73; Maynard-Moody and Musheno 2003, 92; Oberfield 2014). The discriminating research consumer will raise the possibility of social desirability bias in these results, which is a valid criticism and a strong possibility. Even with social desirability bias, however, the pattern suggests that it is normatively better to justify rule-bending for others rather than for oneself.

Discretionary Rule Behavior

Discretionary rule behavior falls outside the boundaries of straightforward rule violations or noncompliance. In the context of organizational rules, discretionary rule behavior arises from an employee's ability to make a decision about rules without consulting organizational authority. Discretionary rule behavior can arise by design or by default. Rules can explicitly grant discretion, as illustrated by some local government rules that allow supervisors and managers to decide whether to

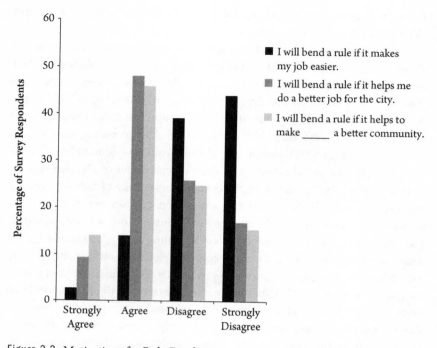

Figure 3.3 Motivations for Rule-Bending
Source: Local Government Workplaces Study, Organizations 1–4, n=646

require a medical note for absences, call a snow day, or allow telework. Discretion by default surfaces when rules are incomplete or vaguely worded or they conflict with other rules. Whether by default or design, discretion functions in a rule's gray zone, where black and white requirements are not available or known.[1]

Discretion is a major theme of the street-level bureaucracy literature.[1] In their overview of this body of research, public administration scholars Steven Maynard-Moody and Shannon Portillo trace the evolution of thinking about discretion (2010). In the past, frontline workers—such as public employees interacting with citizens—were thought to be powerless and lacking discretion. The authors cite pathbreaking research that demonstrates that not only are front-line employees not powerless, they exercise considerable discretion in implementing top-down policies (Lipsky 1980; Wilson 1989). This discretion has positives and negatives. On the upside, rule discretion can create a more flexible and responsive bureaucracy. On the downside, rule discretion can weaken democratic control and "rule of law" and place the most vulnerable citizens at risk of abuse and neglect. The authors dispute the notion that discretion and rules are independent, and they call on further research to better understand how discretion is "nested within rule-based systems."

Employees in the Local Government Workplaces Study provide another view of rule discretion, which employees generally dislike when in the hands of supervisors and managers who are above them in the organizational hierarchy. From this vantage point, managerial discretion evoked feelings of inconsistency, unfairness, and favoritism. One program specialist in the Women, Infants, and Children program explains:

> What makes me mad about the rules is that human resources writes up bylaws, which you call rules. When they write out a rule, at the end of it they'll say, "upon supervisor discretion." So to me that's not making out a rule because you still open up the door for the supervisor to do what she wants to do. So if you are going to make up a rule, you need to make it be where there is no supervisor discretion. That way, when it becomes a problem, we can both refer to the book and get the same answer from the book, as opposed to now, where the book states the rule and also states that the supervisor can make the decision. I think that's unfair coming from the human resources department.

This program specialist echoes a sentiment expressed repeatedly by study participants, especially those in frontline positions: rules that explicitly grant managerial discretion are like having no rule at all. This sentiment provides an interesting contrast to some current government reform thinking, which argues that managers need discretion to tailor solutions to create responsive and efficient government (US National Performance Review 1993; Osborne and Gaebler 1992). Similarly, social work scholars debate whether in practice government reform has stamped out discretion or strengthened it (Evans and Harris 2004). These tensions—between discretion and consistency, fairness and flexibility, autonomy and accountability—are inevitable in all organizational rules.

Enforcement

The enforcement of a rule entails all the preceding rule behaviors and then some. Enforcers interpret rules and decide whether and how to apply them. But enforcers also explain rules to followers, monitor compliance, and deliver noncompliance consequences. On the task of explaining, a building official comments:

> We have folks who don't understand rules, are ignorant of them. We try very hard to explain to folks why you have to do these things. If people understand that having a fence around a pool in the backyard is important because so

many kids die per year drowning in pools, they understand. We give reasons. When you explain rules you get better results.

Explanation is a critical function of enforcement because it allows enforcers to clarify requirements and convey legitimacy to rule followers. Explanation can also have the added benefit of helping enforcers make sense of the rules they are applying. A fire department secretary experienced this as she was explaining travel reimbursement to firefighters: "At first, travel reimbursement forms seemed stupid, but then you see the bigger picture."

Monitoring is also a function of enforcement. Early research on organizational formalization included monitoring as part of its operational definition. In 1966 sociologists Michael Aiken and Jerald Hage used surveys to query social welfare agency employees about rules and enforcement. One survey question asked employees to rate their level of agreement with the statement, "People here feel they are constantly being watched to see if they obey all the rules" (1966, 502). The authors do not provide descriptive statistics in their report, but the same question asked in the LGWS suggests that employees do not perceive extensive rule-monitoring: two-thirds disagree with the statement about being watched for rule violations (Figure 3.4). This pattern is consistent with what SLB researchers have been arguing for years: the limits on human time and attention, particularly in resource-strapped public organizations, make rule-monitoring more theory than practice (Lipsky 1980; Maynard-Moody and Musheno 2003; Prottas 1979; Riccucci 2005).

The SLB literature pays particular attention to rule enforcers. SLB scholars argue that public employees who enforce rules among citizens can make or break rule effectiveness and essentially alter public policy (Lipsky 1980; Maynard-Moody and Musheno 2003). Rule-enforcers can serve as diplomats, representing rules and public organizations in the best possible light. Rule-enforcers can undermine rules by sending verbal or physical cues that signal red tape and pointless bureaucracy. Rule-enforcers can have tin ears, as illustrated by the social welfare worker profiled by Norma Riccucci; the worker insisted on explaining the family cap rule to a woman whose tubes had been tied (2005, 38). All these enforcement behaviors influence the likelihood that rules will be followed or violated and ultimately effective or not.

Across Rule Behaviors
Rule behavior is complex and varied, venturing far beyond images of compliance and violation that marked the early days of rule scholarship. Rules are variably interpreted, depending on the clarity or age of the rule and its compatibility with

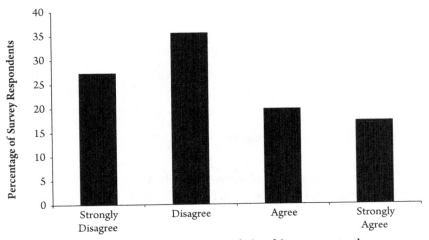

Figure 3.4 Rule-Monitoring
Source: Local Government Workplaces Study, Organizations 1–4, n=637

other rules. Compliance appears to be the most common rule behavior but is not always cooperative in nature: a rule can be rigidly, maliciously, or excessively followed. Rules can be violated to different degrees: sometimes they are bent and other times "snapped in half" (Maynard-Moody and Musheno 2003, 113); sometimes the motivations are prosocial, sometimes malevolent or self-serving. Rule discretion allows leeway—purposefully or accidentally—in how rules are implemented. Rule enforcement entails its own set of activities, including rule explanation, monitoring, and noncompliance consequences. This spectrum of rule behaviors suggests that public employees have a choice in how they respond to rules, and those choices can have positive and negative effects.

Influences on Rule Behavior

What causes rule behavior? The question is important to both practitioners and scholars. Practically speaking, public managers benefit from knowing the roots of rule behavior and give clues about which factors can be manipulated and which are out of managerial bounds. From the scholarly perspective, identifying a diversity of influences on rule behavior enriches our theory, enabling more cross-disciplinary pollination and strengthening the validity of our explanations.

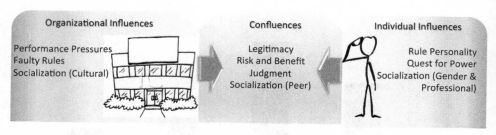

Organizational Influences	Confluences	Individual Influences
Performance Pressures Faulty Rules Socialization (Cultural)	Legitimacy Risk and Benefit Judgment Socialization (Peer)	Rule Personality Quest for Power Socialization (Gender & Professional)

Figure 3.5 Influences on Rule Behavior

This section explores ten influences on rule behavior culled from organizational scholarship and supported with LGWS data (Figure 3.5). Some of these influences, such as rule personality and the quest for organizational power, stem from the individual. Other influences, including performance pressures and faulty rules, derive from the organization. Legitimacy, risk and benefit, and judgment arise from the confluence of organizational and individual forces, while different types of socialization falls into all three categories of influences. We begin with individual influences on rule behavior and the role of rule personality.

Rule Personality

Rule personality is the bundle of individual attitudes, preferences, and beliefs that inform how an employee responds to rules. Two rule personalities surface in popular culture and the public management literature: bureaucratic and unbureaucratic. Bureaucratic personalities are rigid rule-followers who need boundaries and feel adrift when rules are not available to guide behavior (Bozeman and Rainey 1998). Unbureaucratic personalities, by contrast, view rules as optional constraints on their discretion that can be discarded if the situation calls for it (DeHart-Davis 2007; Brockmann 2015). A third type, the "average" rule personality, is introduced here. While not as colorful or dramatic, the average rule personality shows up in the LGWS and, as suggested by the data, is far more common.

Organizational scholars have been portraying the bureaucratic personality in an unflattering light for over half a century. Sociologist Robert K. Merton's bureaucratic virtuoso "never forgets single rule binding action and is unable to assist many clients" (1940). Victor Thompson's variant, the bureaupathologist, is professionally insecure and thus excessively aloof, resistant to change, insistent on status, and ritualistic in attachment to routines and procedures (1977). Barry Bozeman and Hal Rainey's bureaucratic personality is alienated and desires more rules to create the illusion of power (1998). Anthony Downs's conserver—typically a middle manager lacking in promotion potential—avoids rule deviation to protect organizational status (1967). "Complacent" street-level bureaucrats, typically minority or non-college-educated workers, engage in an "acquiescent and unimaginative use of agency procedure" to secure position and occupational status (Stone and Feldbaum 1976).

In an illustration of the bureaucratic personality from the Local Government Workplaces Study, one building inspector talks about a former colleague:

> One guy several years ago thought of the whole code as black and white. It drove him nuts. He was a case; his mentality was that there was right or wrong and no in-between. He was wound tighter than a tick. So we used him. If we had a contractor who was trying to cause problems, we would send this guy out to them. He was a loose cannon and we'd point him wherever we could. Both the contractor and inspector would be mad, but the inspector was right. He had the code. The code might have been illogical in that situation and there may have been a more practical, better way to do it. But for this inspector, there was no way around the code. He had a big ticket book he'd love to keep writing in. I don't know that it helped straighten out the contractor, but we used him as an enforcement tool. He later committed suicide.

The building inspector in this excerpt provides a worst-case scenario bureaucratic personality: someone lacking the capacity to see shades of gray and bordering on madness. This bureaucratic personality is extreme, destructive, and, fortunately, rarely found in public organizations.

The unbureaucratic personality, by contrast, receives more favorable treatment—but less press—in the public management literature. Unbureaucratic personalities are portrayed as competent public servants who bend rules to deliver better public service and who exercise significant discretion to achieve governmental goals (Goodsell 2003, 2014; DeHart-Davis 2007). They are characterized as trailblazing public managers who are entrepreneurial to the core (Diver 1982) and catalysts for government reinvention who decentralize decision-making and increase worker discretion (Frederickson and Smith 2003, 215). Unbureaucratic personalities are vocal (Brockmann 2015) and risk-taking nonconformists (DeHart-Davis 2007; Mulder 1971; Morrison 2006); like Maynard-Moody and Musheno's citizen agents, they bend rules to provide justice (2003, 19). Also falling into this category are rebellious Dutch mental health professionals, who exhibit less willingness to implement new policies

(Tummers 2011), and the "Nevada Four," who violate standard operating procedures (along with strategies) to protect wetlands from the Bureau of Reclamation's stated irrigation practices (O'Leary 2014).[2]

Unbureaucratic personalities in the LGWS are mostly employees rebelling against rules that are perceived as ineffective barriers to job performance. These workers tend toward nonconformity and are quick to acknowledge their independence from the system. To illustrate, one journeyman explains that it is "in his nature" to question rules. Unbureaucratic personalities are also risk-takers, like the street department worker who sneaks out from under his boss's watchful eye to trim trees that hang over a sidewalk, which violates the rule to first obtain permission from property owners. "If my ass is chewed, so be it," he claims with pride.

Between the bureaucratic and unbureaucratic personalities portrayed in the scholarly literature, the average rule personality surfaced in the Local Government Workplaces Study (Figure 3.6). As might be expected, bureaucratic personalities are strongly inclined to believe that rules have a purpose (93 percent) and disinclined to believe that fewer rules would make them more effective in their jobs (63 percent). Unbureaucratic tendencies appear from employees who question rules that have an unclear purpose (86 percent) and who disagree that more rule-following would make their organizations more effective (51 percent).

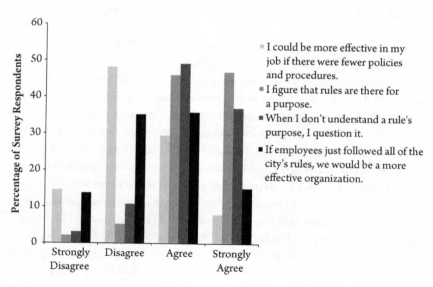

Figure 3.6 The Average Rule Personality
Source: Local Government Workplaces Study, Four Midwestern Cities, n=646

The average rule personality has a healthy respect for rules but is savvy to their limitations.

Employees who respect rules appear to make good employees. Evidence from a 1972 study of private sector employees—taxi drivers, college secretaries, and textile workers—suggests that employees with a higher tolerance for bureaucracy also have better relationships with supervisors, greater promotion potential, and stronger relationships with coworkers (Baker et al. 1973). A more recent study by Jason Dahling and colleagues suggests that supervisors assign lower ratings to the performance of prosocial rule-benders (2012). While unbureaucratic personalities may be desirable for performance jams and bureaucratic personalities advisable during lawsuits, the average rule personality may very well be the crux of effective organizational functioning.

One final thought: Is rule personality born or made? Political scientist Zachary Oberfield provides relevant evidence in a mixed-method study of social workers and police. To understand his subject matter, Oberfield took the unusual step of working for a year as a welfare caseworker while researching his dissertation. He conducted interviews and surveys with social workers and police over a two-year period, comparing how their bureaucratic personalities—which he defines using motivation, attitude, and identity—changed over time. Oberfield found that bureaucratic personality changed some over time, but not much. Organizational socialization appeared to be only modestly influential on personality; more important was the personality that social workers and police brought to the job. Given the role of personality in rule behavior (Brehm and Gates 1997; Kaufman 1960), public organizations should focus on recruiting and retaining employees with personalities that fit organizational needs (Kristof 1996).

Organizational Power

Rule behavior can also be driven by the quest for organizational power. This type of rule behavior is based on the assumption that there is power in knowing the rules (Heidelberg 2015). Three types of rule-based power emerge in the literature: compensatory power, which seeks to overcome a lack of professional or organizational standing; maintenance power, which seeks to retain or expand sources of personal influence; and interpersonal power, which seeks to alter the dynamic of relationships between two or more organization members.

Compensatory power occurs when organization members seek to overcome the lack of professional or personal standing and use rules to exert control over others. In her study of one Fortune 500 company, Harvard business professor Rosabeth Kanter observed some supervisors and secretaries who pursued compensatory power through a rigid adherence to rules, one of their only outlets for personal discretion (1977). Sociologists Joseph Bensman and Bernard Rosenberg identify "downward identification," which is illustrated by low-level officials who cut slack for clients and subordinates in order to empower themselves (1963, 313). Economist Anthony Downs portrays "conservers"—typically middle managers lacking in promotion potential—who follow rules to the letter to protect their organizational positions (1967). In each of these cases, the organizationally powerless engage in rule behaviors that compensate for their own lack of power.

Maintenance power is sought by organization members who use rules to retain or acquire additional power. Melville Dalton's *Men Who Manage* (originally published in 1959) identified supervisors who earned professional props by breaking rules, relying on a personal machismo that demonstrated their skill at end-running the system (2013, 30). Barry Bozeman identifies self-aggrandizement as a source of red tape: the creation of some rules can enhance individual power but contribute nothing to legitimate organizational purposes (1993, 286). Alvin Gouldner's newly appointed plant manager, "Mr. Peele," relied heavily on corporate rules to establish his own legitimacy with the blue-collar workforce and blamed headquarters for the changes in plant operations that he sought (1954).

Rules can also alter the power dynamics of interpersonal relationships, particularly between supervisors and subordinates. Michel Crozier's public employees in France used rules to buffer themselves from authority-laden interactions with supervisors (2009, 55). One supervisor in Peter Blau's study of a US federal agency routinely ignored rule violations in order to later call in favors from rule-bending employees, such as asking work to be completed before deadline (1955, 215). Across multiple study settings, supervisors use selective rule enforcement as a means of currying favor with their employees (Gouldner 1954, 174; Kanter 1977, 193; Crozier 2009, 160; Dalton 2013, 104–7). These cases illustrate the capacity of rules to mitigate or harness authority, to reward or punish employees, and to curry favor and build relationships between individual organizational members—all of which are outside the organizational purposes.

Socialization

Socialization also influences rule behavior. Socialization is both a process and an outcome: people are indoctrinated to believe what is good and right or bad and wrong; if all goes as planned, they emerge from indoctrination holding those beliefs dearly. Four sources of socialization are particularly relevant for rule behavior: from peers, by professionalization, through gender connection, and within organizational culture.

Peers may be the most important source of socialization related to rule behavior (Riccucci 2005). Coworkers signal "peripheral cues" about the rules that can be bent acceptably and under what circumstances. The influence of peers on rule behavior surfaces in study after study: Dutch mental health professionals were shown to be more willing to implement a new reimbursement policy if it was supported by peers and, to a lesser extent, by managers (Tummers, Steijn, and Bekkers 2012); MBA students presented with various scenarios of rule-bending coworkers were more likely to engage in rule-bending themselves (Morrison 2006); social workers who valued their peer relationships indicated a lower likelihood of falsifying paperwork (Brehm and Gates 1997); and gypsum mine employees chastised their colleagues who broke rules by smoking in the presence of an inspector (Gouldner 1954, 186). Peer influences are so significant that they pose a significant challenge to managerial control (Sandfort 2000; Riccucci 2005).

Professionalization is another source of socialization. Professional employees are "preprogrammed" through education or training, which typically occurs prior to organizational entry (Perrow 1986, 128). Local government managers are inculcated to playing roles as community members, regulators, and service providers (Hayward 2010). The forest rangers who embrace compliance with US Forest Service procedures (Kaufman 1960); the nurses who questions rules that do not serve human values (Hutchinson 1990); and the local government employees with strong public service identities who are less likely to bend rules (DeHart-Davis 2007) all have been professionally socialized to rule behavior.

Of course, professionalization can conflict with an organization's rules and create a competition between standards. Gouldner's study of university faculty found that "cosmopolitans"—those with lower organizational loyalty, greater commitment to specialized skills, and identification with an external referent group—had less respect for formal controls than "locals"—those with higher organizational loyalty, less interest in specialized skills, and lower identification with an external referent group. But professionalization does not always run counter to rules. Organization behavior scholars Dennis Organ and Charles Greene found that rules helped clarify roles and strengthened organizational identify among scientists and engineers (1981). Gloria Engel observed that physicians working in moderately bureaucratic settings perceived greater autonomy than those working in nonbureaucratic settings (1969). Professionalization moderates rule behaviors but not necessarily in a straightforward or predictable manner.

Gender is another socializing influence on employees (Mills and Murgatroyd 1991). Beginning in childhood, males and females receive a variety of signals on how to behave (Gilligan 1982): girls learn that they should be cooperative, nurturing, and passive; boys learn that they should be independent, assertive, and in control. These gender expectations translate to rule behavior and explains the tendency for organizational women to exhibit more rule abidance than their male counterparts (Portillo and DeHart-Davis 2009; Portillo 2012; Tyler and Blader 2005; Brehm and Gates 1997; Reason et al. 1990; Morrison 2006) and for organizational women to articulate an appreciation for bureaucratic values (DeHart-Davis 2009b). With greater understanding and acceptance of transgender public employees, it is unclear how these society norms—and the rule behaviors they trigger—will shift.

Organizational culture also socializes employees on acceptable and unacceptable rule behaviors. Culture is the set of "values, beliefs, and assumptions" shared by organization members (Denison 1996, 624). Culture is difficult to measure (Khademian 1997) but critical for effective organization members to be able to identify it (Deal and Kennedy 1982). Every conceivable aspect of an organization provides clues to its culture: from the organizational chart to the configuration of the reception area, the hallway chatter to official organizational language, the website to the office. Employees glean signals from their experiences within the organization, these signals inform their rule behaviors.[3] To illustrate, consider that a "developmental" culture—one that emphasizes organizational learning and embraces risk-taking—is associated with less perceived red tape (Pandey and Moynihan 2005). Not surprisingly, organizational cultures that value rule-abidance have less rule-bending, while cultures that emphasize teamwork and organizational mission have more rule-bending (Borry 2013).[4]

An explanation for rule behaviors related to socialization is the logic of appropriateness. This idea was devised by sociologists James March and Johen Olsen (2006) as a way of explaining human behavior beyond individual calculations of risk or benefit (discussed in the next section). According to the logic of appropriateness, behaviors arise in response to three questions: What situation is this? Who am I in this situation? and, Given the situation and my role in it, what is the right thing to do? The logic of appropriateness belongs to a body of theory called new institutionalism, which defines itself as "a perspective on how political life is organized, functions, and changes in contemporary democracies" (Olsen 2008, 192). Institutions are not physically located, with four walls and a roof, but rather are "enduring collections of rules and organized practices embedded in structures of meaning and resources that are relatively invariant in the face of turnover of individuals and changing external circumstances." This makes for an extremely broad unit of analysis, one that has been questioned for its utility (Goldmann 2005). Nonetheless, the logic of appropriateness makes sense as a narrative of rule behavior: employees respond to rules based on an assessment of context, a reflection on the role they are playing within that context, and their appropriate behavior in light of context and role.

Risk and Benefit

Some scholars portray rule behavior as a clear-minded calculus by individual employees of the risks and benefits of following or breaking rules (Battmann and Klumb 1993). These scholars explain the world as the interaction of principals and agents, with principals delegating to agents, who act on behalf of principals (Jensen and Mecklin 1976). Public managers and employees are one type of principal-agent relationship; others include political officials and bureaucrats and public organizations and contractors. Using a principal-agent approach, expectations of noncompliance punishments or compliance rewards drive rule behavior (Brehm and Gates 1997, 49).

Noncompliance consequences play a role in a variety of rule behavior studies. Political scientists John Brehm and Scott Gates observed that social workers who predicted punishments for rule violations were less likely to violate rules (1997, 125). Psychologist Rebecca Lawton observed shunters—railroad workers who separate and join railroad cars—were slightly less likely to violate safety rules when they perceived safety risks in doing so (1998). Management professors Leslie Sekerka and Roxanne Zolin found that Department of Defense employees who professed rule-following also perceived a greater threat to their workplaces in doing so. From the Local Government Workplace Study, one deputy sheriff comments that, "Rules are like an umbrella. As long as you stay under it, the rain bounces off you. Otherwise, you get criticism and lawsuits."

While noncompliance consequences can influence rule behavior, the influence is limited when rule violations carry little consequence. This tendency toward rule nonconsequence has been observed in a wide array of organizational settings, from narcotics law enforcement (Manning 1977) to safety rules (Reason, Parker, and Lawton 1998) to minority contracting (Terman 2016). Given that rules are mostly followed in public organizations, detecting and punishing noncompliance becomes an ineffective investment of managerial time. Nonconsequences for rule violations become standard rather than the exception and the principal-agent approach inadequately explains rule behavior.

Legitimacy

Legitimacy is another motivator of rule behavior. As previously discussed, legitimacy is the perception of authority as "appropriate, proper, and just" (Tyler 2006). Legitimacy is psychological and subjective: it resides in the minds of those subject to authority. Thus, perceptions of authority comprise the entirety of legitimacy, and perceived legitimacy is redundant.

Legitimacy greases the wheels of cooperation by allowing employees to cooperate with authority without sacrificing their own identities. Social identity relates to how people define themselves and interpret their own standing and worth compared to others (Tyler and Blader 2000, 143). When authority is construed as good, right, and just, it poses no threat to or conflict between individual identity and compliance: authority deserves to be obeyed, and obedience does not imply lower worth or standing within the organization. Illegitimate authority, by contrast, suggests that individual organizational members lack the power to resist organizational injustice. Pushback becomes more likely as compliance appears to jeopardize self-respect.

The link between rules and legitimacy dates back to Max Weber's writing in the early 1920s (1947a, 332), which identified written rules as a dominant feature of rational legal authority and one of three sources of voluntary submission to authority. Organizational rules convey legitimacy by projecting authority that is neutral; they impose neither favor nor bias on individual organization members. This neutrality is to authority as sugar is to medicine: one makes the other easier to take. This remedy stems from the tendency of organization members to distinguish between neutral and biased authority through the lens of their standing and value within the organization. Organization members who perceive authority to be neutral have no need to question their standing or value, given that they are subject to the same requirements as everyone else and that the requirements that were formulated are based on organizational goals and not on individual beneficiaries. Biased authority works in the opposite fashion: by producing handpicked winners and losers, the latter are more likely to question the meaning of such differential treatment and their own individual standing and value to the organization.

The written aspect and inscribed form of most organizational rules in particular conveys neutral authority and thus legitimacy. Writing has a "vatic quality" that appears simultaneously commanding and disconnected from particular individuals and situations (Ong 2013, 78). By comparison, the speech used to communicate unwritten rules is inextricably linked to individual speakers and less capable of appearing impartial. Drawing on social identity theory, compliance with unwritten rules can threaten the self-image of organization members by raising doubts: Is this rule legitimate? If I comply, am I a doormat? By contrast, the impartiality and authoritative appearance of written rules makes them appear *prima facie* legitimate and impartial and enables rule followers to comply without compromising their own sense of standing within the organization. The neutrality of written rules and the effect on compliance echo the work of Mary Parker Follett (2015), Pauline Graham (2003, 121–39), and Chester Barnard (1938), all of whom argue that neutrally perceived authority is more likely to induce cooperation from compliant parties than authority perceived as arbitrary, personal, or biased.

The perception that written rules are neutral authority also aids enforcement efforts. Enforcement in most modern public organizations does not occur by brute force but rather through cooperative interactions between rule-followers and rule-enforcers. Whether through the provision of access and information, acknowledgment of infractions, or acceptance of noncompliance consequences, this cooperation depends on the perception that such efforts are impersonal and sanctioned by organizational superiors. Such perceptions reduce the conflict that can occur in interactions between followers and enforcers and disagreements over the validity of rule violations or negotiations regarding compliance consequences. Such conflicts are more likely to arise with unwritten rules, which cannot provide evidence that rule-enforcers have been authorized to implement rule provisions (DeHart-Davis 2009a). In these cases enforcement appears unfair because it lacks advanced warning (Gouldner 1964, 168).

One public works secretary interviewed for the LGWS illustrates the role of rules in neutrality, identity, and, ultimately, legitimacy:

> A good rule is our snow removal policy . . . Before it snows, we line up the materials, labor, and routes, all planned for the good of the city as a whole. This prioritized order determines the routes, with residences last . . . Citizens are not happy with the order, even though I explain it to them. Why don't you plow driveways, they ask? One person even accused us of intentionally plowing snow on her driveway, even though she was "the best citizen on the block." I can refer citizens to our procedures and show that they are not being picked on.

The secretary's comments underscore the importance of and mechanisms for creating legitimacy. First, she references the process undertaken by the city to devise the plowing policy, for the purpose of determining what was "good for the city as a whole" rather than for particular citizens or groups. Second, she notes that a citizen accusing the city of plowing snow onto her driveway referred to herself as "the best citizen on the block," which demonstrates how people compare identities when it comes to rule behavior: this citizen construed herself as a better citizen than her neighbors yet on the losing end of the rule implementation. Third, the secretary used the plowing rules (which are posted on the city's Web page) to show citizens that the rules are neutrally derived and that no one is "being picked on" and thus, in essence, legitimate.

In prior research, Tom Tyler and Steven Blader also linked legitimacy to three types of rule behavior: self-reported compliance with organizational policies, deference to organizational policies, and rule-breaking (2005). Their research conducted survey data from two samples, the employees of a US branch of an international finance firm and a group of Internet-recruited respondents. In both samples the legitimacy of authority increased rule-deference and compliance and lessened rule-breaking. Thus, theory and evidence support the prominent role of legitimacy in rule behavior. (We will revisit the implications of legitimacy for the design and implementation of effective rules in the next chapter.)

Performance Pressures

A variety of performance pressures also affect rule behavior. These pressures arise from the requirement to work quickly and process volumes of people and tasks, sometimes in the face of voluminous and rapidly changing rules (Sandfort 2000). If rules are perceived as a hindrance to accomplishing work objectives, they are more likely to be violated than those that pose no such barrier (Lehman and Ramanujam 2009). Consequently, technicians will repair moving equipment to maintain production (Dalton 1987, 82); employment agents will forgo career counseling to quickly process high volumes of low-skill textile jobs (Blau 1955, 26); and flextime employees of the Department of Defense will be "no-show" during requisite office hours because they are working at other times in order to avoid interruptions that might preclude timely completion of work tasks (Sekerka and Zolin 2007).

When performance pressures produce psychological stress, rule behavior can also signal coping. In this new strand of public administration research, public management scholar Lars Tummers and colleagues analyzed fifty-seven studies related to how employees use rules to deal with intense workloads and citizen demands (2015). Their analysis detected three coping strategies: moving toward, moving away from, and acting against. *Moving toward* can involve rule-bending to benefit citizens; *moving away from* shifts citizen attention to the rules as a way of achieving psychological distance; and *acting against* entails rule rigidity and aggressive behavior toward citizens. While the research is still in the developmental stage—and neglects the role of emotional labor—these categories are valuable for understanding how rules are used to combat psychological stress and provide both positive and negative organizational effects.

Faulty Rules

The management literature is chock full of rules being bent or broken because they are poorly designed, are thoughtlessly implemented, or contradict organizational mission. From the LGWS, the comments from one nurse in a county health department illustrates:

> Sometimes the rules that they make at the health department are not conducive to accommodating the client. Right now I do refugee processing. I interview refugees first, then I decide which clinic they should go through. That's time-consuming and can't be done all at once. The refugees don't speak English, so they need an interpreter service. If there is a family of seven, it will take a good hour before you can get them processed. They need a tuberculosis screen and stool sample for parasites, then we schedule them for physical assessments. The first day I'm with them three and a half hours. All their kids are with them. Right now I'm scheduled until September for doing initial interviews. Refugees get Medicaid, which is good for eight months from when they arrive in the US. It takes six months to complete the immunization process. If it's two months before I see them, they will lose their Medicare. Them going through that red tape, it should never be like that. So I talked to the supervisors at the clinics and they agreed to let them walk in when it's convenient for them. Also, I divided the processing up into two visits so that families would not have to be here so long.

The nurse in this example engages in a process called "task revision," by which employees alter procedures perceived to be faulty (Staw and Boettger 1990). She arranges for walk-ins rather than appointments and she splits client processing into separate visits so that refugee families don't lose their Medicaid benefits because of system inefficiencies. Scholars have observed task revision among nurses who bent rules that were perceived as interfering with their ability to care for patients (Hutchinson 1990) and among railway shunters who violated safety rules under tight time frames and heavy workloads (Lawton 1998).

Faulty rules can trigger task revision in a variety of ways and with measurable effects on rule behavior. Rules that are voluminous and rapidly changing are subject to selective enforcement (Sandfort 2000, 736). Highly detailed rules are susceptible to rule violation because they are hard to follow (Reason, Parker, and Lawton 1998) and easy to break (Prottas 1979). Rules perceived as red tape (that is, burdensome and ineffective) are associated with more favorable attitudes toward rule-bending (DeHart-Davis 2007). Rules that pit organizational values against one another are more likely to be violated (Reason, Parker, and

Lawton 1998). Rules that emphasize procedural requirements over substantive outcomes are less likely to be implemented as planned, such as State of Florida policies that sought to encourage purchasing with minority vendors (Terman 2013). Rules formulated without employee input—and those that allow little implementation discretion—can be alienating to employees and reduce the likelihood of cooperative implementation behavior (Tummers 2012). These snippets of research reflect a broader trend in organizational research toward a focus on how rules can erect barriers. The next chapter flips the coin and explores rule attributes that enable action.

Judgment

Employees sometimes bring to bear their own judgment in deciding how to respond to a rule. The role of personal judgment in rule behavior is inevitable, borrowing modern philosopher Immanuel Kant's sentiment that there is no rule for following rules (Kant and Guyer 1998, 268). The need to exercise judgment can be triggered by rules that explicitly allow discretion but also by rules that provide incomplete or ill-fitting guidance for the situation at hand. Three types of judgment are particularly relevant to rule behavior: experiential, moral, and situational.

Experiential judgment draws on personal experience, on-the-job training, and trial and error. From the LGWS, one police officer provides a colorful example of experiential judgment and its implications for alternative rule behaviors:

> One radio station decided to send naked strippers to give out popsicles at construction sites. The DJ gave the site location over the radio and citizens called in. Newer cops were sent and they cleared the strippers [from the area]; a couple of girls were even arrested. Older cops would have made the girls go inside so that citizens wouldn't see them. They also wouldn't have arrested the strippers. What's the point of that? It gives the city police a bad rap to be heavy-handed.

From the police officer's perspective, newer police officers had less experience upon which to draw in identifying alternative courses of action. The newbies took the path of greatest resistance: collaring strippers rather than sending them on their way, which only served to intensify the conflict rather than diffuse it, and ignored the impact of such actions on the police's relationship with the community. From this seasoned officer's perspective, more-experienced officers would have considered organizational values they understood but that were not explicitly covered in the rulebook and they would have taken alternative actions.

Herein lies the essence of experiential judgment: time on the job yields knowledge that transcends the rulebook. This is not to say that experienced employees will more often bend the rules. Indeed, the literature on experience and rule-bending is inconclusive. Psychologist James Reason and colleagues found that younger people violate drivers' safety rules more than older people (1990). By contrast, survey participants in the LGWS expressed slightly more liberal attitudes toward rule-bending the longer they had worked for cities or counties. And Zach Oberfield's study of police officers and social workers found that bureaucratic personality (including attitudes toward rules) remained relatively stable over several years beyond initial job orientation (2014).

Moral judgment yields decisions based on a personal sense of right and wrong. In a study by Steven Maynard-Moody and Michael Musheno, frontline public employees—cops, teachers, and social workers—used moral judgment to determine whether citizens were worthy of rule-bending or rule-following (2003). Determinations of worthiness were based on perceived sincerity, cooperativeness, likelihood of change, and respect for the agent's authority. These findings led Maynard-Moody and Musheno to conclude that frontline employees can strengthen their moral reasoning, and thus rule decisions, by sharing stories and reflecting on their meaning for citizen services.

Situational judgment occurs when employees decide to bend or break rules based on the characteristics of the situation at hand. Public management scholar Alexander Henderson observed situational judgment in his study of paramedics (2013), in which medical protocols sometimes conflicted with patient needs (resulting in, for example, more narcotics than allowed being given to patients in extreme physical and emotional pain). Sociologist Peter K. Manning observed the same situational judgment in his study of two narcotics units of the London metropolitan police (1977). In London the funds available to make undercover drug purchases were governed by written rules that were routinely broken, depending on the size of the bust, the prominence of the drug dealer, and the track record of the informant facilitating the sale. Manning found that pre-approval processes were rarely followed because drug sales moved rapidly and entailed varying levels of risk and payoff that had to be considered when deciding whether or not to follow the rules.

From the LGWS, one firefighter illustrates situational judgment as applied to the rules for entering a burning building:

> Sometimes you may have a rule to follow, but the situation dictates that you break it . . . It's a matter of judgment. But if you've ever won an award, you've probably broken a standard operating procedure.

From the firefighter's perspective, the characteristics of the fire itself—who is in the burning building, where the flames are most intense, how rapidly the flames are spreading—must be considered when making decisions about whether standard operating procedures apply.

Whether experiential, moral, or situational, judgment is an inevitable contributor to rule behavior. Some judgments will produce rule behaviors consistent with organizational objectives; other judgments will produce rule behaviors that are inaccurate, inappropriate, or organizationally damaging. Public organizations that acknowledge the role of judgment in rule behavior have a better chance of influencing it, whether through training, continuing education, or socialization.

Influences on Rule Behavior

Rule behaviors emerge from a complex web of individual and organizational influences. Personality alters attitudes toward and reactions to rules. The quest for organizational power can drive behavior and result in rules being used to compensate for powerlessness, maintain existing power, or alter interpersonal power dynamics. Socialization—the process and outcomes of indoctrination—makes certain rule behaviors more desirable than others. Perceptions of risks and benefits motivate or deter particular rule behaviors. Legitimacy influences rule behaviors by casting authority as valid or invalid. Performance pressures and faulty rules can constrain rule behaviors, making compliance unrealistic under certain circumstances. Judgment brings individual decision processes to bear on alternative rule behaviors.

These ten influences have been explored as if they were independent, when in reality the strands of the behavior web are intertwined: socialization inevitably influences judgment, personality informs risk-benefit calculi, and faulty rules lower their legitimacy. Additionally, not all influences are susceptible to manipulation. Some, such as rule characteristics and performance pressures, are amenable to organizational engineering, while others, including personality and gender socialization, lie outside managerial reach. Whether within or beyond organizational reach, public managers should be aware of these influences, both to understand the limits of rules and the need for voluntary cooperation.

Summary

There are many ways in which rules can be acted upon, along with a spectrum of influences on rule behavior. Rules are interpreted and enforced, with more or less discretion. Rules can be followed or violated, not as opposite actions but rather as distinct types of behavior with their own variants and consequences. The many influences on rule behavior arise from a complex cauldron of individual and organizational influences, with some amenable to managerial manipulation and others outside managerial control. The sheer range of rule behaviors and influences illustrates that employees are not passive recipients of organizational structure but rather active contributors to the functionality of an organization's rules.

Notes

1. Evelyn Brodkin and Malay Majmundar write about "procedural discretion," a term they use to describe the discretionary requirements that a caseworker can impose on clients, "when they demand face-to-face meetings beyond those required by regulation, [they] set appointment times without regard to claimant circumstances (such as pickup schedules for school children), or [they] schedule multiple claimants simultaneously, producing long waiting times at welfare offices" (2010). Procedural discretion in this sense flows from the power of the caseworker to impose burdensome requirements and not on the discretion arising from the rule itself.

2. One interesting departure from the portrait of the heroic rule-bender is sociologist Victor Thompson's bureautic (presumably rhyming with neurotic). The bureautic is immature and insistent on immediate gratification, that is, childhood traits not outgrown in adulthood. Given that this person detests being controlled, organizational life is torturous and all organizational demands are perceived as red tape. Rules and processes remind the bureautic that he or she is not in control and is dependent on others. Characterized by low levels of abstraction and a preference for personalized relationships, the bureautic cannot understand the need for rule requirements and interprets them as impugning on his or her trustworthiness and dignity. The bureautic does not bother to learn rules or their purposes and, as a result, constantly violates them (Thompson 1977, 175).

3. See Franklin and Pagan 2006 for formal and informal sources of organizational culture.

4. Erin Borry's research measures ethical climate, or employee perceptions of work climate relevant to ethical decision-making (2013).

CHAPTER 4

The Rules Framework and Grievance Policies

Let us consider how the organization rules framework applies to the case of non-union employee grievance policies.[1] The framework identifies three perspectives on rules: organizational, individual, and behavioral. The *organizational* perspective surveys the role of rules in enabling goal-oriented organizational action. Rules can more or less coordinate, empower, and constrain; they convey specific behavior expectations; they socialize to values and norms; and they store knowledge and signal legitimacy. The *individual* perspective explores the ways that rules are experienced as empowerment, constraint, and legitimacy but also as procedural fairness, trust, organizational identification, and status-leveling. The *behavioral* perspective shifts attention to the actions taken in response to rules. Rules are interpreted, enforced, followed, and violated with more or less discretion. Shades of behavioral gray reside in each of these categories, making rule behavior highly varied and complex.

Employee grievance policies are an ideal case for the organizational rules framework because they involve a diverse set of stakeholders, including city and county managers, attorneys, human resources staff, department heads, and employees. The chapter begins with the organizational perspective, which emphasizes grievance policy function (to reduce employee lawsuits and symbolize employee voice) and form (to coordinate, control, and empower; store learning; and legitimize). The individual perspective comes next, exploring how grievance policies empower some employees and constrain others (sometimes leveling social status and at other times reinforcing it and alternately evoking and suppressing procedural fairness and trust). The final section delves into the behavioral perspective and examines the range of rule behaviors that can be triggered by grievance policies.

The evidence presented comes from a 2014 study of North Carolina cities and counties funded by the Local Government Research Collaborative (LGRC).[2] LGRC is a network of over twenty local governments and universities nationwide that invests in academic research to shed light on effective city and county management. The study sought to identify patterns of grievance activity, common grievance policy designs, and the effects of grievances on organizational outcomes. Interviews were conducted by phone and in person with twenty North Carolina local government managers and human resource professionals to generate background information on grievance processes in the state. Surveys were also used to collect quantitative data on grievance processes, grievance rates, and related managerial systems.

The Organizational Perspective and Grievance Policies

Grievance policies first surfaced in public and private organizations in response to President Woodrow Wilson's War Labor Board, which gave workers the right to organize and collectively bargain but not strike (Gregg 1919; US DOL 1922; Freidin and Ulman 1945). Private organizations, hoping to head off unionization by employees, formed company-run unions that oversaw employee grievance processes (Edelman 1990). Thus grievance policies originally served as a way for companies to reduce the likelihood of union formation.

The dramatic expansion of individual employee rights over the past fifty years has spurred a simultaneous expansion of grievance policies in both public and private organizations (Colvin 2003).[3] Public organizations use grievance policies to accomplish several goals, starting with the management of legal risks that arise from workplace conflict. Grievance processes typically trigger internal investigation of such conflicts and allow public organizations to determine whether conflicts are attributable to mistakes by managers, by employees, by bad rules, or from some combination of the three. This due diligence helps public organizations decide whether to respond in favor of the employee(s) by diagnosing and possibly repairing offending managerial mistakes; by vetting the strength of their own prospective legal defense (in cases of employee error); or through some combination of legal defense and organizational development (i.e., revising rules or clarifying processes).[4]

Along with managing legal risk, grievance policies are used to coordinate an organization's framework for its reaction to workplace conflicts. Deadlines are set for different steps in the process and delineate a certain number of days for employees to grieve, for departments to respond, and for conflicts to be resolved. Employees are given the opportunity to tell their side of the story, usually at a conference or hearing. Restrictions are imposed on who can and cannot be present during such conferences or hearings: human resource managers are almost always present, coworkers and private attorneys less often so. In most public employment grievance processes, workplace conflicts are handled through mediation, external review by a civil service commission, or peer review. Supervisors and managers are typically prohibited from retaliating against grieving employees. Written petitions and responses can be required, which enable a track record that the organization can use to evaluate any evidence submitted and buttress its legal case. Each of these elements orchestrates the organizational response to formalized workplace conflict.

Along with risk management and coordination, grievance policies are used to empower and constrain managers and employees. Conventional wisdom holds that managers are more constrained by grievance policies than employees. Managers must respond to grievance claims in writing and adhere to deadlines for doing so, and (in some cases) they are prevented from attempting to informally resolve problems with grievants. Employees, conversely, are empowered by the availability of a process that gives them an outlet for voicing their concerns (Edelman 1990; Klaas and Denisi 1989). In particular, grievance policies provide a process by which employees can bring wrongs (perceived and real) to the attention of upper management to be heard and addressed, in most cases without fear of retaliation (DeHart-Davis, Maynard, and McDougall 2015).

Like all organization rules, grievance policies enable learning and store knowledge. Organizational learning can arise during the design of a grievance policy, through the involvement of multiple perspectives and stakeholders. Grievance policies also offer learning opportunities during the implementation of rules, through the internal investigations triggered by grievance processes. Grievances can reveal managerial "hot spots," or those supervisors or policies that create the most conflict. The information gleaned from grievance processes can feed back into organizational development and inform process and managerial improvements, such as revised rules on the interpretation and implementation of a given policy.

As a repository for organizational knowledge, grievance policies contain specific elements that reflect prior organizational experiences. A local government's previous experience with grievance cases can inform departmental deadlines: a prior sexual harassment lawsuit may spur a provision that allows employees to bypass offending supervisors in the grievance process. Or employee perceptions that grievance policies are sham processes can lead to the use of peer-review panels. In each of these cases, elements of grievance policies reflect an attempt to capture the lessons learned from a tangible prior event.

The knowledge capacity of a grievance policy depends on the frequency at which it is revised. Two findings from the North Carolina study provide evidence for this proposition. First, the average grievance policy age is nine years, suggesting that grievance policies tend to be revised infrequently. Second, survey respondents who reported knowledge of newer grievance policies also tended to perceive those policies to be more effective. (Conversely, older grievance policies were perceived as less effective). These results are consistent with the argument that rules reflect organizational learning and must be refreshed to remain useful (March, Schulz, and Zhou 2000; Beck and Kieser 2003; Kieser and Koch 2008).

An organization's desire to appear legitimate to internal and external stakeholders also drives grievance policies (Edelman, Uggen, and Erlanger 1999; Haraway 2005) and responds to the need to look good and right in the eyes of the public, the media, and elected officials. Grievance policies convey legitimacy by mimicking legal processes in the resolution of workplace conflicts, including specific procedural steps, the presentation of evidence, and a hearing for the employee (Haraway 2002). This process signals to employees, elected officials, and the media that the public organization is a just employer that is willing to hear employee perspectives on workplace conflicts and subject itself to internal legal requirements.

Of course, the legitimacy of a grievance policy can be undermined if a public organization uses it to justify unjust actions toward employees or to pay lip service to employee concerns. Regarding the latter, the depth and breadth of grievance investigations vary greatly by organization: when only lip service is being paid, grievance policies are "myths" that are symbolic but devoid of sincere intent (Meyer and Rowan 1977). The possibility of this happening is easy to imagine but difficult to establish empirically. In the North Carolina data reported here, on average 75 percent of grievances are resolved in favor of managers rather than employees. This lopsided result has several possible explanations. It could be that only the worst employees file grievances or, alternatively, that employee grievances are a mixture of valid and invalid complaints that are vetted in a system specifically designed to maintain existing managerial power structures (Haraway 2005). If the latter, grievance policies project a false sense of rationality and fairness that can backfire on an organization and create adversarial relationships between managers and employees and lower employee morale (Haraway 2002).

Grievance policies also socialize employees to organizational values and norms. One former assistant city manager illustrates the socializing capacity of grievance policies in his "zero-fault approach," which automatically resolved grievances in favor of the employee if managers had committed any procedural errors. The manager created the process because supervisors were not following their own rules, which caused a spike in grievances and a rise in employee distrust. In creating this zero-fault approach, the manager communicated to both managers and employees the importance of employee worth, procedural fairness, and organizational trustworthiness. The result was a small but perceptive shift in organization culture, after which grievances declined by half in the subsequent two consecutive years.

Looking across rule functions, grievance policies serve organizational rationality by managing legal risk. They constrain managers from treating employees illegally or unjustly and empower employees to voice their concerns when they suspect illegal or unjust treatment. Grievance policies coordinate organizational responses to workplace conflicts and reflect the "sheet music" effect of rules. They convey the legitimacy of the public organization and demonstrate its conformity to legal and social norms. Finally, grievance policies allow public organizations to learn from workplace conflicts and store that learned knowledge through policy revision.

The Individual Perspectives on Grievance Policies

Grievance policies can evoke a range of individual experiences vis-à-vis an organization's rules. Employees can be empowered or constrained, depending on grievance process design and implementation as well as the employee's organizational position. Social status can be rendered moot by grievance processes, such that no hierarchical position is immune to organizational justice (though, as we will see, the evidence of success is mixed). Grievance policies are supposed to impart procedural fairness, convey legitimacy, and build trust, but they can fail at these tasks if management always wins, supervisors break rules with impunity, or the organization appears overly preoccupied with managing legal risk. We begin with the capacity of grievance policies to empower and constrain.

Empowerment and Constraint

Generally, grievance policies seek to empower employees and constrain managers. Employees are empowered by having access to a process for protesting adverse personnel decisions. Without a grievance policy, employees typically have no formal internal opportunity to contest unfavorable employment decisions. Even sham grievance policies can be empowering, by allowing aggrieved employees to rattle managerial cages, stir up the legal staff, or generally "stick it to the man."

Managers are the true target of most grievance policies. Walking in the manager's shoes: a grievance policy allows an employee to publicly file a complaint against you. Even the most outrageous claim can be articulated in the context of a forum covered by the media. Managers are at risk of being quoted as having said and done things that, even if patently untrue, will live into digital perpetuity. Many grievance policies prohibit retaliation and sometimes circumscribe communications with employees once a grievance has been filed.

But grievance policies can also work in the opposite fashion, constraining employees and empowering managers. Grievance policies that are difficult to understand discourage complaints; deadlines can be tight, paperwork onerous, and processes intimidating. While grievance policies generally empower, they can be designed to do so for only the most outraged and highly motivated employees.

The majority of grievances tend to uphold management action: in the North Carolina study, 75 percent of grievance outcomes upheld management decisions. This pattern raises a question: Do grievance policies stack the deck against employees? Or do they simply ferret out bad employees, especially those most likely to cause trouble when held accountable for workplace misdeeds? Surely the truth lies in the middle, but without knowing the answer to this question it is hard to know the extent of inherent managerial empowerment or constraint in grievance policies. Only the possibilities can be speculated.

Empowerment and constraint each have organizational advantages and disadvantages. Empowerment can be positive, giving employees voice and boosting morale. Empowerment can also be negative, incentivizing employees to complain about every minor workplace conflict. Constraint can be positive, making managers think twice about treating employees poorly; it can be negative when it discourages managers from addressing performance problems. While popular management trends evaluate empowerment as "good" and constraint as "bad," empowerment and constraint have no inherent normative value in the context of grievance policies.

Status-Leveling

Grievance policies also illustrate the potential for rules to level the organizational status of people from different social strata. This is one of the original benefits of bureaucracy observed by sociologist Max Weber: bureaucracy applies rules to everyone, not just the king's favorites or the priest's groupies. Grievance policies enable lower-level employees to air complaints against their managers, typically for adverse employment actions such as firing, demotion, or suspension. In theory, no hierarchical position is immune from grievance.

Do grievance policies truly level status? At a minimum, grievance processes empower lower-level employees to articulate their concerns, to call out managers, or to "rattle legal cages." Beyond making noise, the answer is unclear. David

Lewin and Richard Peterson found that grieving employees in four organizations—a steel manufacturing firm, a retail department store, a nonprofit hospital, and a local public school district—tended to have lower performance evaluations, spottier attendance records, fewer promotions, and higher turnover rates after submitting grievances than did their nongrieving counterparts (1999). In the North Carolina study, cities and counties with higher grievance rates also had higher turnover rates and about three-fourths of grievance outcomes upheld management decisions (DeHart-Davis, Maynard, McDougall 2015).

The implications of this evidence for status-leveling depend on interpretation. If grievance processes tend to attract the worst employees, then higher turnover rates, lower performance evaluations, and management "wins" makes perfect sense. But if grievance processes elicit a mix of good and bad employees, then one would at least expect a higher percentage of employee wins, because "nobody bats a thousand," as one corporate manager in David Ewing's 1989 study commented. Without knowing the quality of employees who grieve, the question of status-leveling remains unanswered.

Procedural Fairness

On the face of it, grievance policies embody the concept of procedural fairness when people believe that decision processes are unbiased and neutral (Feuille and Chachere 1995). Recall the two theoretical influences on procedural fairness: voice (when people are able to provide input into decisions that affect them) and process characteristics (which raise the likelihood of unbiased decisions). In theory, grievance policies are designed to deliver both. Grievance policies give voice to employees who suspect that they have been subjected to unjust adverse employment decisions. Voice arises from the ability of employees to file formal appeals, present evidence, and have that evidence heard by a third party who has the power to potentially overturn the decision. As for process characteristics that lead to procedural fairness, grievance policies seek: consistent application across people and time through written requirements; the suppression of bias by excluding from the decision-making process the supervisors and managers against whom grievances have been filed; and accurate information, through the submission of evidence from multiple parties. Bad decisions are correctable in that final decision makers can overturn adverse employment actions already taken. The ability of an employee to be represented by legal counsel or accompanied by friends or family increases the diversity of perspectives considered.

The story of one fire department provides an interesting illustration of how grievance policies can go awry and be construed as procedurally unfair.[5] A television station reporting on employee claims stated that fire department managers were not responding within required time frames; that requests for representation at meetings were being denied; and that investigations were occurring without employees being asked for their versions of events. In response to these allegations, two grieving employees made the following comments:

> "When [employees] file a grievance it's just really wanting to know that they are heard and there are two sides to every story."

> "It's not just a job to them . . . Those people are important and they should be valued."

Regardless of the truth of the allegations of the news story, the comments of the employees illustrate that grievance policies can effectively—or ineffectively—communicate the inherent value of the employee and the just nature of the employer. In the fire department case, some employees perceived the opposite: a poorly implemented grievance policy had both devalued them as employees and portrayed their employer as fundamentally unjust.

Legitimacy

Recall that employees deem rules to be legitimate if those rules are perceived as "appropriate, proper and just" (Tyler 2006). Most rules appear legitimate because they are written, the writing of which suggests that they have been fashioned neutrally, applied without bias, and signify "the weight of the organization" (McPhee 2004). Regarding grievance policies specifically, legitimacy is conveyed by providing a neutral process for the resolution of employee disputes with management, especially that the process is applied without bias and with the sincere intent of giving a voice to employees over the workplace issues that affect them (Haraway 2005).

But grievance policies can be implemented in ways that violate these principles and sabotage legitimacy. The most common threat to legitimacy is the appearance of a "rubber stamp" process: when grievance policies *always* uphold management decisions, it suggests that the deck is stacked in favor of management and that grievance processes are a waste of employee time. Another source of illegitimacy in grievance policies arises from managers who violate grievance policy requirements with impunity, such as managers who fail to communicate with employees by the grievance policy deadline. Grievance policies can also appear illegitimate when they appear to focus primarily on protecting the organization from legal liability to the exclusion of delivering procedural fairness or giving employees voice.

Trust

Like all organization rules, grievance policies can maintain or erode trust between employees and managers. Recall that trust involves the belief that another party will do as promised and cause no harm in the process. Rules alter trust through the levels of control that are imposed, through the organizational competence being demonstrated (or not) by the rule, and by the extent to which rules are consistently applied.

Grievance policies add a few twists and turns to the notion of trust. They help maintain trust when designed to give employees voice and rectify organizational injustice; when they require managers to follow their own rules; or when employees win every once in a while. Grievance policies erode trust when they uphold status quo power structures and never find in favor of employees. It is unclear whether grievance policies can truly build trust. The same characteristics designed to further the appearance of legitimacy—the requirement of evidence and hearings and win-lose outcomes—are the same ones that pit employees against managers in a quasi-legal win-lose setting. Sim Sitkin and Robert Bies label this phenomenon "the formalization paradox" (1993, 30), wherein rules that are designed to foster trust ultimately create conflict and adversity.

Looking across individual perspectives, grievance policies can be experienced as a form of employee voice or as a testament to the preordained power structure. Grievance policies that provide a fair hearing for adverse employment actions, that sometimes find in favor of employees, or that subject all layers of the pecking order to standards of organizational justice, give employees voice. By contrast, grievance processes that feign employee voice, stack the deck in management favor, or do not require managers to follow their own rules, simply uphold existing power structures.

Behavioral Perspective on Grievance Policies

Grievance policies are designed to trigger a predictable set of organizational behaviors in response to employee charges of unfair treatment. Employees start the process by filing a written complaint that voices their concern(s). Managers are given a deadline to confirm receipt of the grievance. A fact-finding investigation typically commences. Some policies call for the involvement of a third party (upper management, a personnel board, or a peer review panel) to take information and decide the outcome, whether in favor of the employee or manager. If all goes well, the organization determines its culpability and the employee receives a fair hearing.

While the process may appear impersonal, grievance processes exact a high emotional toll on participants. Most have a quasi-legal feel that produces winners and losers and pits employees against managers. Even when management decisions are upheld, grievance processes can embarrass managers by calling into question their supervisory judgment (Ewing 1989, 9). Managerial fears of this type of scrutiny can lead to two types of rule behavior: greater rule-following, to reduce the likelihood of being accused of inconsistent rule application, and greater rule-bending, because employees are not held accountable for compliance. Note this example from William Haraway's research of grievance processes in the Commonwealth of Virginia:

> A seasoned manager who trains employees in grievance handling for a large [public] agency in the commonwealth summed up this point: "The instant reaction of supervisors [to a grievance] is defensive. . . . Supervisors feel threatened and fear what will happen to them. They are scared to death of their employees and terrified of their bosses." (Haraway 2002, 512)

When supervisors fear employee grievances, it can lead them to avoid conflicts with employees, including those related to rule-enforcement. Thus the supervisor must make a judgment that evokes a principal-agent challenge: Is the benefit of enforcing this rule worth the risk of enduring a grievance process?

Rule-following and rule-bending can also be used as a way for managers to punish grievants, following the notion that rule behavior can be driven by personal interest. One way of doing so is to stringently enforce the maximum time frame for grievance filing. To illustrate, consider a policy that requires employees to file a grievance within a fifteen-day window of the event (the most common time frame among North Carolina local governments). The manager informs the employee on day sixteen that she is out of luck: the window of opportunity for seeking corrective action has closed.

Managers can also ignore their own deadlines, as alleged by the local television news story discussed earlier. In this instance, a fire department employee quit and then filed a grievance. Her supervisor was supposed to acknowledge her grievance within three days, a time frame that came and went. From the employee's perspective, she was left dangling in limbo, not knowing whether her complaint would be answered or if she had just joined the ranks of the unemployed.

Managers can also punish grievants by retaliating, a rule-breaking behavior expressly forbidden by most grievance policies. Retaliation is suggested— though not proven—by lower performance ratings and promotion rates and higher turnover rates among grieving employees (Lewin and Peterson 1999). In the North Carolina study, local governments with higher grievance rates also had higher turnover rates. Indeed, half of the employees surveyed in one study perceived retaliation to be a real possibility (Drost and O'Brien 1983).

While managers are responsible for most rule behaviors in grievance processes, employees are not passive participants. Some employees inevitably follow the grievance policy in good faith and hope for the best. But not all employee complaints are made in wisdom or good faith. The availability of a grievance policy can lead some employees to overuse the system and file unwarranted nuisance grievances, particularly when a wide range of workplace issues are grievable. In one example of misplaced conflict, an employee in Haraway's study of grievance policies in Virginia notes:

> I filed a grievance . . . to the issue [of an incorrect leave balance] directly to my supervisor. He was very detached about it. I just wanted an apology [for my leave balance being calculated incorrectly]. He said there would be no apology by the clerk who made the mistake. I then took the written grievance to the second-step-level manager. He yelled at me and was mad that I even sent it to the second step. Finally, he said he'd try to arrange the required grievance meeting. But weather prevented the meeting and I agreed to extend the required time limit for the meeting to take place. That was February [more than a year ago]. I haven't heard a word since. It tells me how things go around here. The grievance has never again been mentioned [by my supervisor]. If it had been a more important issue to management, they would have treated the grievance more seriously. (Haraway 2005, 335)

It is unclear why an employee would file a grievance to get a paperwork correction and apology. Yet this type of minor grievance filing is not completely absent in the public sector workplace. One interviewee for the North Carolina study of counties had previously worked for a city in which grievances were the rule rather than the exception. From the manager's perspective, two factors contributed to a perfect storm of conflict: workplaces that were very centralized and hierarchically structured, with dictatorial supervisors and voiceless employees, and (perhaps in response to the first factor) a personnel oversight board that was entirely sympathetic to employees and loathe to uphold managerial actions. The city's grievance process became the illogical but predictable venue for resolving workplace issues that could have been better addressed elsewhere (e.g., in supervisory training, an employee forum, or workplace studies).

Malicious compliance is another way that employees can react to grievance policies. One Virginia employee interviewed by Haraway illustrates:

[Management] is gathering information as much as it can. I don't give them much. It is gathering information so it can devise a strategy on how to get around it [the grievance] . . . so what I usually do in the body of the grievance where it says factual basis for the grievance, I write in there — "we will discuss it here [at the grievance meeting] if need be," and don't put anything else in there. I put a very simple [explanation and as] few words as possible. (Haraway 2005, 336)

In this example, the employee follows the letter of the rule by filling out the form. But the spirit of the law is being violated and information is not being shared in good faith. This is the essence of malicious rule compliance.

Many of the precursors ascribed to rule behavior apply to grievance policies as well. The most important of these is legitimacy, which influences the likelihood that employees will use grievance processes. Remember that legitimacy derives from the perception that organizational processes are neutrally derived and fair. If managerial decisions are always upheld, if employees suspect retaliation, or if supervisors do not follow their own rules, then legitimacy takes a nosedive and grievance policies rust like a quaint antique on a restaurant wall. But other precursors apply as well. Grievance policies themselves can alter rule behavior by being complicated or simple and easier or harder to understand and thus more or less likely to be used.

Grievance policies evoke a range of potential rule behaviors. When followed in good faith by managers and employees alike, grievance processes can effectively manage legal risk and impart fair treatment. However, other rule behaviors can derail grievance policy objectives. Supervisors can decline to enforce other rules to avoid grievances, can rigidly apply grievance time frames, or can break with grievance policy and retaliate against grievers. Employees can clog the system with nuisance complaints and not cooperate in fact-finding investigations. As with any rule, public managers should think about the potential behaviors that a grievance policy can trigger instead of assuming that rules will be followed and enforced as written.

Summary

The review of non-union employee grievance policies puts flesh on the bone of the organizational rules framework. The organizational perspective focuses on how grievance policies coordinate an organization's response to workplace conflicts; they empower, constrain, and socialize organizational members; they enable learning and store knowledge; and they legitimize the organization to the public, to the media, and to elected officials. The organizational perspective, while necessary, does not capture the ways in which individual organization members experience grievance policies: as signals of procedural fairness, trust, and legitimacy; as reflections of individual standing and worth; as a window of understanding into the true nature of the organization. The behavioral perspective adds a third lens to the mix: grievance policies trigger managerial actions and employee responses—including willful rule-bending and uncooperative behavior—that alter rule effectiveness.

Several themes have surfaced in this analysis that pave the way for understanding effective organization rules. As grievance policies demonstrate, rule effectiveness cannot be defined from the organizational perspective alone: effective rules must also look through the individual and behavioral lenses to anticipate how people will perceive and actively respond. A broad swath of stakeholders can make or break grievance policy effectiveness, suggesting that stakeholders must be considered in rule design and implementation. And grievance policies have both technical and social components, following legal models of decision-making but requiring employee and supervisor cooperation in order to function smoothly. These themes will be addressed as we consider how public organizations can create effective rules.

Notes

1. "Non-union" is an important qualifier here, given that grievance policies are a permanent fixture in union environments: collective bargaining agreements mandate processes by which employees can fight managers and possibly reverse adverse employment decisions. Grievance policies in non-union environments—such as the North Carolina local governments studied for this chapter—lack the teeth of union grievance processes and evoke a different context for studying rule implementation and design. To avoid verbosity, this chapter uses the term grievance policy to refer to grievance policies in non-union environments.

2. Research design details can be found in the final report to the LGRC by DeHart-Davis, Maynard, and McDougall (2015).

3. Public employees are protected from unlawful search and seizure and guaranteed certain types of free speech. They are protected from discrimination (as are all employees) based on a range of criteria, including but not limited to gender, race, religion, national origin, military status, and genetic predisposition.

4. In theory, legal risk is managed by grievance policies through the internal resolution of conflicts between employees and managers (Yenney 1977). According to this explanation, grievance policies ensure that all positions receive "fair and careful consideration" (Haraway 2002, 43) and that unjust employer actions can be reversed.

Extant research suggests that the claim is dubious: grievances tend to fracture workplace relationships, uphold management decisions, and trigger higher quit rates (Lewin and Peterson 1999). In the case of the LGRC study, local governments in North Carolina with higher grievance rates also have higher turnover rates, which further undercuts the notion that grievance processes resolve conflicts (DeHart-Davis, Maynard, and McDougall 2015).

5. See the story at http://www.wsoctv.com/news/news/special-reports/9 -investigates-city-employees-call-grievance-proce/njFpQ/.

CHAPTER 5

Creating Effective Rules through Green Tape

Effective organizational rules are no small matter, given the intensely challenging public sector environment. Public organizations are under siege politically and economically, battered by antigovernment vitriol yet expected to deliver high performance and operate with razor-thin budgets. With few resources for recruiting and retaining employees, rules have become a ubiquitous element of the public sector environment that affects employee morale (DeHart-Davis, Davis, and Mohr 2014). Despite the stereotype of the rigid, unresponsive bureaucracy, in public organizations rules are critical for achieving efficient and effective workplaces. In short, effective rules in public organizations are vitally important, now more than ever.

This chapter explores how public organizations can design and implement effective organizational rules. The first order of business is to reconceptualize rule effectiveness by drawing on the implications of the organizational rules framework. In determining when rules should be written, the case is made for involving stakeholders—those who explain, enforce, and comply—in rule design. Diving into the weeds of rule creation, a section on green tape theory identifies five attributes of effective rule design and implementation. Green tape theory is applied to the five-second rule, a legally doomed informal policy of Missouri police in the wake of the 2014 Michael Brown shooting. Finally, red tape and green tape theories are compared for their respective contributions to understanding the effectiveness of rules. As will be seen, effective organizational rules do not emerge by accident but require focused managerial time and intention.

Reconceptualizing Rule Effectiveness

Public management scholars have traditionally defined effective rules as those achieving organizational purposes. Considering the organizational dimension of the rules framework, this definition makes perfect sense: rules are effective to the extent that they accomplish what public organizations intend. However, the individual and behavioral perspectives of the framework suggest that people are not passive recipients of organization structure; rather, they are active participants in creating the realities around it. Rules create relationships between people and organizations that transcend the rule itself. Rules can be followed or violated in ways that support or undermine their purpose and alter organizational effectiveness. Thus, rule effectiveness needs to be thought of more broadly: as achieving organizational purposes but also as a vehicle for eliciting voluntary cooperation through interactions between the individual and organization.

Organizational purposes must be front and center in conceptualizing effective organizational rules. This seems like an obvious proposition, but in reality it is a challenging one. Most organizational rules do not include written objectives. Even when objectives are explicit, rule outcomes (like other forms of public sector performance) are notoriously hard to measure (Head and Alford 2008). Sometimes rules arise from unclear and contradictory aims (Kaufman 1977, 11; Bozeman and Feeney 2011, 68) or values that are extrinsic to core missions (Baehler, Liu, and Rosenbloom 2014). Nonetheless, public organizations generally know when rules work, such as when employees follow social media guidelines, learn the travel reimbursement system, or interact with citizens in a positive way.

Another essential element of rule effectiveness is the *voluntary cooperation* of those expected to follow, enforce, and explain organizational rules. The behavioral dimension of the rules framework demonstrates that people can react to rules in a variety of ways that either support or undermine rule objectives. Even when rules are mostly followed, they can be rigidly or maliciously complied with, as well as bent or broken. It is not enough to command compliance; as social psychologists have long argued, cooperation is easier and more efficient than coercion (Tyler 2006). Indeed, many counterproductive rule behaviors arise from a coercive managerial mentality of favoritism, micromanagement, or unrealistic performance pressures, to name a few. Thus, effective rules must be defined by the extent to which they elicit voluntary rather than coerced behavior.

Interaction is the final element of the revised conceptualization of effective organizational rules. Rules are points of interaction between employees and organizations that can affect organizational effectiveness, but these effects traverse far beyond the narrow confines of the rule. Rules empower and constrain employees, speaking volumes to an individual's value, standing, and trustworthiness. Procedural fairness, legitimacy, and status-leveling alternately cement or fracture the emotional connection between employees and their organizations.

These interactions between people and with the organization spark the level of cooperation with a rule likely to be achieved, as well as the sheer capacity of the organization to achieve the purpose of the rule and beyond.

This conceptualization of rule effectiveness moves away from a command-and-control conception of rules and places employee reactions front and center. This is a departure from Weber's idea of a rule, as an impersonal instruction executed by a cog in a wheel (Senigaglia 2011). Rule stakeholders—those who explain, enforce, and comply—must be ready and willing to cooperate. To create willing rule-followers requires a different kind of public organization, one that is more empowering and less controlling than the rigid hierarchical structures of yesteryear.

When to Write a Rule

Ultimately the decision to write a rule is a matter of managerial judgment. There is no algorithm that will automatically slot problems into the "write a rule" or "leave it be" column. Nor does guidance on rule-writing leap from the pages of scholarship on organizational effectiveness. Rather, it must be inferred from both the scholarship and common sense, which together identify two conditions for effective rule-writing: significant organizational problems with reasonably clear causes.

Scholars of organizational learning suggest that rules arise in response to problems that have not been adequately addressed by other rules (Schulz 1998; March, Schulz, and Zhou 2000). Organizational problems cover a wide range of territory. Some are internal and are created by undesirable behaviors and human error. Others derive from external forces—government regulation, public opinion, or liability—that create financial, legal, or reputational issues if left unresolved.

Over time, organizations respond to problems by creating more rules (positive density dependence), which solve increasing numbers of problems so that fewer new rules are needed and the rate of rule-creation decreases (negative density dependence; Schulz 1998). A study of academic and administrative rules at Stanford University bears out the argument: rules increase over time, but at some point their growth rate slows down (March, Schulz, and Zhou 2000). An analysis of Dutch "rules" on national laws pertaining to higher education over a forty-year period also supports the positive density dependence model (van Witteloostuijn and de Jong 2009).

From the Local Government Workplaces Study, a municipal fleet manager illuminates the practical aspects of rules as problem solvers: "When there's an issue or problem that we've dealt with collectively, and people are still coming into my office with problems, that's when I have to write a policy."

Problems alone are not enough to prompt this manager to write a rule; it is problems that involve multiple people and for which solutions have been attempted. This insight jibes with Schulz's argument that rules are likely to be written when problems are "'fairly recurrent, consequential, or salient'" (Schulz 1998, 848).

The notion that certain problems—those that are recurrent, consequential, or salient—are well-suited for rule-writing can be used as a practical guide for avoiding writing rules in response to extreme events, to a handful of people, or even to a particular employee. Such unwarranted reactions are a contributor to red tape because they create rules that serve political symbolism more than managerial pragmatism (Bozeman 2000; Bozeman and Feeney 2011).

Reasonably certain solutions are the second condition for effective rule-writing. "Reasonably certain" is an important qualifier here, because human beings have not yet aced the art of predicting behavior. All rules contain behavioral forecasts, yet those forecasts are rarely 100 percent accurate (Bozeman 2000). Prospective rule solutions do not require dissertation-level analysis but they do need to express a common-sense relationship between rule requirements and objectives.

Appropriate rule-writing also depends on the clarity of organizational goals and the availability of technical knowledge for problem-solving. Public management scholar Hal Rainey cites the Social Security Administration's file tracking system as one example. SSA "wanted more efficient, effective file tracking procedures. In addition, the consultants had well-developed ways of analyzing the efficiency and effectiveness of the new file tracking system. A rational procedure served very well" (Rainey 2014, 188). When organizational goals are murky and technical knowledge is limited, Rainey argues, other forms of decision-making will emerge, including "bargaining and political maneuvering and more intuitive, judgmental decision making" (188).

When should rules be left unwritten? Flipping the conditions for written rules, unwritten rules are well suited for unimportant problems and unclear solution sets. Another possibility is that unwritten rules are more desirable when managers seek flexibility for solving problems. The LGWS data bears this suggestion out: unwritten rules are perceived as more flexible (see Figure 5.1). The correlation is not terribly strong, but statistically significant nonetheless ($r = 0.10, p < 0.01$). Truth be told, scholars have a long way to go in understanding unwritten rules before this question can be answered. The importance of the informal organization rule has long been acknowledged (see Blau and Scott 1962

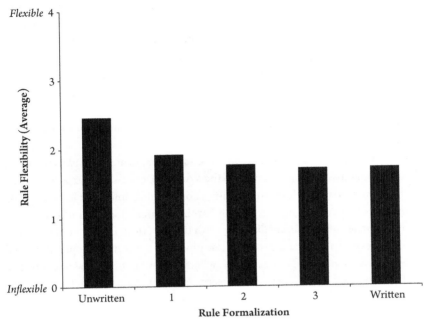

Figure 5.1 Rule Formalization and Flexibility
Source: Local Government Workplaces Study, Organizations 1–4, n=630. Based on survey responses to the question, "How would you characterize rules in your workplace between the following opposite characteristics?"

for an overview), but scholars have yet to dive deep into the nature and consequences of unwritten rules, partly because they are harder to observe and study systematically.

Rule Stakeholders

Cooperative behavior is essential for effective rules. The most cleverly designed rule will fail if there are not people willing to follow, enforce, and explain the rule's requirements. Achieving effective rules requires actively incorporating the experiences, understandings, and beliefs of those whose cooperation is required.

Involving stakeholders in rule design is a logical starting point but no small order to fill. Public administration scholar Camilla Stivers observes how public employee voices are sometimes marginalized in decision-making despite the fact that they are "experts on the conditions of their own lives." Commenting on media coverage of pre-9/11 airport screening flaws, she writes:

It is amazing how frequently experts underrate or even ignore what people know about a situation just from living in it. A few days after September 11, 2001, a *New York Times* story carried this headline, "Even workers can see flaws in airlines' screening system." *Even* workers! Why is this such a surprise? Who would know the flaws in the system better than the screeners themselves? Yet until disaster struck no one asked them how things were going, and of course overworked and poorly paid people were hardly going to volunteer information, especially when they were likely to get blamed for whatever was wrong.

What if, instead of investigating the screeners, someone had asked them to help figure out ways to improve the system? Out of direct experience and facts amassed through scientific study, people build democratic knowledge by means of discussion and argument. Yet this is rarely done. Somebody has to take the fall, after all. One difficulty with the American representative system of government is that it provides few pipelines for conveying people's lived experiences into the policy process, whether they are firing line workers, like the airport screeners, clients of the service delivery system, or citizens in general. (2008, 134)

Stivers's argument captures the single most important step that public organizations can take when designing an effective rule: solicit the input of people most affected by the rule, whether those people are employees, businesses, or citizens. Without such input, public managers will be crafting rules in a vacuum and without a full understanding of what rules will mean or how they will affect the people or the situation.

The idea of stakeholder input is relevant today but by no means new. Since the era of parasols and topcoats, management scholars in the human relations tradition have recommended the involvement of key stakeholders in the design of organizational processes. Mary Parker Follett, an early scholar of human relations thinking, tells the story of "a lady who posted over the sink in her kitchen the proper sequence of dishwashing":

Her cook did not say what she felt about it but a few days later she put her own feelings into the mouth of someone else by saying, "Mrs. Smith's cook came to see me yesterday and she said she wouldn't have that in her kitchen."

This instance throws some light on, also, what I have said on the advantage of the rules of the job being the outcome of joint study. If this lady had said to her cook and maids, "Let us think out the proper sequence of dish-washing and then stick it [up on the wall], all might have been well perhaps. There

would have been nothing to resent if they had a share in making these rules."
(Graham 2003, 132)

Setting aside the gendered white-lady nature of the example (which is remark-
able, given the 1926 audience of white male managers), Follett is arguing that
organizational rules will work better if employees are involved in rule design.

A second justification for stakeholder involvement in rule design is to close
the design-implementation gap that is created when rule-designers and rule-
followers are two separate groups of people. A public works director illustrates
this gap:

> This lawyer and I worked for two years on a codebook that deals with the
> water utility to convey authority and responsibility to the water supervisor.
> These are general, broad policy guidelines. The former version of the code-
> book included mandatory operating hours and a requirement to use copper
> piping. The legal staff were emphatic that the copper piping requirement stay
> in. I ask, "Why?" They told me, "This means you can use copper piping." He
> didn't understand that we don't need to use copper piping anymore, it's an old
> technology.

The design gap in this example is attributable to a mismatch of expertise. Without an engineer at the table—one who understood the best available technology
for water delivery—lawyers were left to devise solutions that did not fit the situation at hand. The potential for means and ends to be mismatched shrinks when a
broader range of stakeholders can contribute to rule design. Barry Bozeman uses
a similar approach in his suggestion that public organizations should conduct red
tape audits in which rule-stakeholders jointly review policies and ferret out red
tape (2000, 176).

A third rationale for stakeholder involvement in rule design is the potential for
greater compliance from rule-followers (Adler and Borys 1996). Safety scholar
Mathilde Bourrier relays the importance of buy-in for extremely high compliance rates at a nuclear facility called North Anna, where rules changed constantly based on worker input. The ability of employees to request rule changes
meant that there was no reason to circumvent the rules. "This greater degree of
involvement increased their commitment, and hence, their compliance" (Bourrier 1999, 46).

Stakeholder involvement in rule design also strengthens the relationship
between managers and employees. Public management scholar Ellen Rubin
found that Department of Defense employees that have the opportunity to

weigh in on workplace decisions perceive those decisions as more procedurally fair, which in turn links to higher job satisfaction and lower turnover intentions (2007). Stakeholder involvement in rule design also builds trust between managers and employees by allowing employees to protect their own interests, to minimize the risk of opportunistic manager behavior, and to demonstrate trust and respect for employees (Whitener et al. 1998). Alvin Gouldner referred to rules that were designed by both employees and managers in a gypsum mining company as "representative bureaucracy," which produced rules implemented with wide support and minimal conflict (1954, 216).

Of course, not every rule stakeholder will want to participate in rule design, as Michel Crozier pointed out in his commentary on French bureaucracy (2009, 205). While employees interviewed for the LGWS could quickly identify bad rules and knew their opinions of good rules, not one said, "I'd really like to be on the committee that takes this rule apart." But there are ways for savvy managers to maneuver around this hesitancy. Barry Bozeman suggests creating the "oligarchy of the interested" by soliciting volunteers among employees interested in rule design (2000, 17). This approach is promising but risks "garbage-can" decisions, whose quality depends on who shows up and which axe they are grinding (Cohen, March, and Olsen 1972). Another approach suggested by Ronald Mitchell, Bradley Agle, and Donna Wood is to select stakeholders with power, legitimacy, and an immediate stake in the game (1997). One local government took this approach in revising its personnel policies (see Box 5.1). As organizations move toward more employee-centric workplaces, stakeholder involvement will increasingly be construed as part of the job for both managers and employees.

Green Tape: Attributes of Effective Rule Design and Implementation

Beyond rule creation, rule effectiveness, and rule stakeholders, attention must also be paid to the nuts and bolts of effective rules, referred to here as "green tape." Green tape is a grounded theory of effective organizational rules based on the lived experiences of public employees and their encounters with rules.

The idea for green tape emerged from the Local Government Workplaces Study. The study was designed with red tape in mind, based on the assumption that cities and counties are an ideal laboratory for studying ineffective, burdensome rules. To avoid anchoring interviewees on the term "red tape," employees were asked about examples of good and bad workplace rules, including why they labeled rules as such. The interview data were then analyzed for patterns that could provide clues about rule effectiveness and ineffectiveness. This grounded

Box 5.1 Employee-Driven Policy Design

One town included in the Local Government Workplace Study provides a model for involving rule stakeholders who are employees. The town's organizational development coordinator began a series of meetings with employee groups as soon as town administrators knew they would be revising policies related to the Family Medical Leave Act and Worker's Compensation. Each meeting involved an update to employees about the status of the policy-in-development and collected comments on the draft rules. In addition to the in-person meetings, employees were able to comment on draft versions of the policies both electronically and on paper. (The organizational development coordinator created a notebook of proposed policy revisions, along with sticky notes for the less-than-tech-savvy employees to weigh in on policy design.) This process produced policies that were implemented with minimal disruption to the organization because employees were already familiar with pending changes and felt greater ownership in them. Employee-driven policy design is a form of procedural justice through which employees perceive policies as fair, in part because they are given a voice in the process.

theory approach (Glaser and Strauss 1999) gave voice to public employee perceptions as opposed to fitting employee perceptions into preexisting theory.

The interview data revealed five rule attributes that were identified by local government employees as key contributors to rules perceived as good or bad: rule formalization, rule logic, consistent application, optimal control, and rule understanding. These attributes were mapped onto the existing literature, with the expectation that they would interact and influence one another in predictable ways (DeHart-Davis 2009a, 375). The term "green tape" was chosen to provide a language for expressing effective rules in contrast to the red tape concept. Green was chosen because it provides a vibrant stop-and-go comparison to red tape. (Public management scholar Barry Bozeman originally suggested the term "white tape" to capture beneficial rules [1993], but white lacks the visual punch and counterbalancing effect of green.)

Beyond identifying specific characteristics of effective rules, green tape theory makes a broader point: that effective rules—ones people will follow—possess both technical and social components. A well-designed rule with no followers is as ineffective as a poorly designed rule faithfully followed by all: both fail the organizational intent. This angle returns us to the needed reconceptualization of effective rules: rules that are designed to achieve specific organizational purposes (the technical components) involve interactions between individuals and organizations that elicit more or less voluntary cooperation (the social components).

The following section examines each green tape attribute and how each contributes to effective rules. The section concludes by applying the green tape framework to the "five-second rule," an organizational policy used by police in Ferguson, Missouri, for crowd control in the wake of a fatal police shooting. The analysis illustrates what happens to an organization's rules in the absence of all five green tape attributes.

Rule Formalization

Rule formalization—both the process and outcome of putting rules into writing—is expected to increase the technical and social merits of an organizational rule. This statement will seem circular to those who believe that only written rules can truly be considered rules. But unwritten rules commonly exist in public organizations simply because not every organizational preference can be expressed in writing (Barnard 1938, 172). Some unwritten rules that surfaced in the LGWS include: no more than two employees can take vacation at one time (small work unit); employees are allowed to work at home up to two days per week; unit managers must report a detailed log of work performed by unit employees; all travel vouchers for the previous month must be turned in by the tenth of the month following the travel; dress code requirements; and an employee who no-shows to work three times is automatically terminated.

Given that rules can be both written and unwritten, the green tape framework suggests that written rules are more effective. Participants in the LGWS appear to concur: the more workplace rules are documented in writing, the more they are perceived as being effective (see Figure 5.2). There are two possible reasons for this. First, rule formalization triggers in-depth thinking about the design of the rule, to a higher degree than unwritten rules are capable of generating. As mentioned early on, the sheer act of formalization is inherently more transparent and more amenable to the input of a range of stakeholders. Unwritten rules, by contrast, typically originate in one person's mind (usually the manager's) and thus are less transparently formulated and harder to evaluate. This argument is supported with evidence: written rules are generally perceived as being more logically designed than unwritten ones (DeHart-Davis, Chen, and Little 2013).

Legitimacy is the second reason for the relative superiority of written over unwritten rules. Having written rules legitimizes implementation and makes the rules easier to follow and enforce. Written rules correlate with more favorable attitudes toward rule compliance (DeHart-Davis 2009c) and lower rule-bending

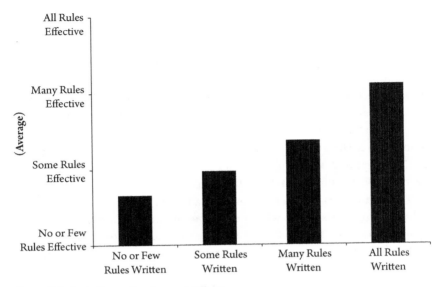

Figure 5.2 Rule Formalization and Effectiveness
Source: Local Government Workplaces Study, Organizations 8–9, n=624

(DeHart-Davis, Chen, and Little 2013). The results of two experiments found that MPA students and public works managers were significantly less likely to bend unwritten rules over written disciplinary rules (Borry et al. 2016). The bottom line, drawn by theory and common sense, is that written rules carry more weight with employees than unwritten rules do, and public organizations should consider this fact when deciding how to translate important behavioral preferences into action.

Written rules are also raw material for enforcers, legitimizing authority, downplaying personal power, giving fair warning, and assigning blame to management for unpopular requirements (Perrow 1986, 26; Gouldner 1954, 166). These functions are particularly critical for rule enforcers who lack built-in societal status, such as women, minorities, and young people. Shannon Portillo's research on authority and rules is instructive on this point (2012). When interviewing city administrators and police officers, Portillo heard from women, minorities, and young people who relied on rules to legitimize their authority. This was not so true with older white men, who perceived rule reliance as evidence of weakness and something to be relied upon as a last resort. Thus women, minorities, and the young face a paradox: they need to rely on rules to legitimize their authority but are perceived as weak when doing so.

Rule Logic

Logic is at the core of rational thinking and a necessary attribute of green tape and contributor to the organizational dimension of rule effectiveness.[1] The rationality of any organizational activity can be evaluated as to whether there is a logical connection between the activity's design and its purpose. Such a connection does not necessarily involve exhaustive empirical analysis; it simply must display a *prima facie* connection between organizational means and ends. This is a good thing, given that ends are difficult to measure in public organizations (Lan and Rainey 1992; Head and Alford 2008). Logic does not need to be determined solely by organizational elites either; the front lines of the organization may be the most adept at sniffing out breakdowns in causal assumptions.

The idea that an effective rule requires a logical design is not new. Flawed behavioral forecasts—erroneous predictions about human responses to rule requirements—are identified as a key contributor to red tape (Bozeman 1993, 2000). Inaccurate assumptions about cause-and-effect relationships explain how some rules are violated (Jackson and Adams 1979; Blau 1963). Rules can impose unnecessary constraint and yield control when management (in the form of "gambling, exploration, and adventure") is needed (Landau and Stout 1979). Accuracy—using the best available information in decision-making—is a criterion for procedural justice (Leventhal 1980). And cognitive adequacy, which is theoretically required for effective formalization, includes error-free abstractions (Stinchcombe 2001). These concepts are variations on the principle of rule logic.

An example rule with faulty logic can demonstrate this premise. In the past, the US Federal Aviation Administration required ticket agents to ask airline passengers two questions: (1) Has anyone unknown to you asked you to carry an item on this flight?; and (2) Have any of the items you've been traveling with been out of your immediate control since the time you packed them? The FAA began asking these questions in response to a few early incidences of passengers carting dynamite-laden luggage on board to generate life insurance money for relatives (or for themselves, if sneaking dynamite in a relative's luggage) (Price and Forrest 2016, 53). After the 9/11 terrorist attacks, Transportation Security Administration secretary Adm. James Loy dropped the requirement, which he labeled "stupid" because it had not prevented the attacks (Brill 2003, 572; Carpenter and Pena 2008, 246). The rule was not necessarily stupid as much as it was questionably illogical.[2] While one can argue in favor of the face value of the rule—that such queries could have lowered the likelihood that a Trojan bomb would be brought aboard by sensitizing passengers to the whereabouts of their luggage—there is no evidence (indeed there is counterevidence) that the logic of the rule did not hold up during implementation.

Consistent Rule Application

Consistent rule application, the third attribute of green tape, figures into all three perspectives of the organizational rules framework. Consistency is not about rule rigidity but rather avoiding systematically exempting specific people or groups from the rules intended to cover them. Occasional rule exemptions are part and parcel of managerial discretion. But frequent and patterned rule inconsistency undercuts organizational purposes, alters individual perceptions, and triggers uncooperative rule behaviors.

From the organizational perspective, consistency serves the rationality function of rules by rendering behavior predictable and coordinated in the pursuit of organizational goals (Weber 1947a; Hummel 2007). From this perspective, rules are akin to a vaccination that is only as good as the spatial coverage of the population that receives it. For example, if all city departments except public works apply the sexual harassment policy, the city administration is still vulnerable to lawsuits and culpable for an ethical lapse in this one unit. Returning to the vaccination analogy, inconsistent rule application is akin to gaps in immunization coverage: where certain groups of people are not vaccinated, health policy goals are not achieved among those populations. Similarly, where well-designed rules are not implemented, organizational goals embedded in rule preferences are not achieved.

Consistency is a powerful dimension of the individual perspective on organizational rules. Rules applied to some people or groups and not to others inform perceptions of the extent to which the organization is procedurally fair. Procedural fairness is a concept tied closely with social identity theory: employees look for cues in the workplace environment to interpret their standing and worth within the organization (De Cremer and Tyler 2005). In practical terms, employees who are subject to rules when others are not tend to ask themselves, "Why me/us and not her/them?" Rule inconsistency thus alters the relationship between the individual and the organization by acting upon employees' belief in procedural fairness and social identity.

Rule consistency also informs rule behavior, as evident in the work of political scientists John Brehm and Scott Gates (1997). Drawing on psychology research, they note that people make decisions based on past behavior by themselves or others. Past behavior is one type of "peripheral cue" that serves as a shortcut for decision-making. Extending the idea of peripheral cues to rule behavior, Brehm and Gates note that the consistency of rule application leads people to decide to follow rules or not. One experimental study bears this out: public works managers who were told that a rule was consistently applied by fellow supervisors were more likely to follow that rule, regardless of whether the rule was written or unwritten (Borry et al. 2016).

Consistency in the application of rules conceivably runs counter to contemporary messages of customer service and decentralization, which suggest that the most effective public organizations must be flexible, agile, and responsive. This train of thought argues that managerial discretion is the key to effective public management, as opposed to rules that summon the ghosts of Frederick Taylor's theory of scientific management and Luther Gulick's POSDCORB steps in the administrative process. In the case of responsiveness, if discretion involves exempting particular individuals or groups, then managers should be prepared for the consequences, including the negative implications for legitimacy and procedural fairness. As will be seen, the five-second rule demonstrates precisely why consistency is a critical modern management concern and a necessary attribute of effective rules.

Optimal Control

It is easy to think of control in negative terms and the means by which managers coerce employees into desirable organizational behaviors. This idea emphasizes how rules minimize discretion and standardize organizational behavioral but in the process trigger inefficiency, morale problems, and counterproductive work behaviors. Control is typically conceived as one-dimensional and without layers or nuance or purposes beyond coercion. Indeed, most organizational scholars envision control in this way (Adler and Borys 1996).

However, rules impose more than one level or type of control, with both positive and negative consequences. It is useful to think of rules as residing on a continuum, from inadequately controlling to excessively controlling, with the sweet spot of optimal control somewhere in the middle. This is the approach of green tape theory, which identifies optimal control as one of the five characteristics of effective organizational rules that contribute to technical capacity and stakeholder cooperation. To see how optimal control contributes to green tape, let's consider the continuum of rule control and its effect on organizations, individuals, and behavior.

At one end of the continuum lies under-control, which imposes a level of constraint that is inadequate for achieving rule objectives. Under-control is problematic from all three perspectives of the organizational rules framework. For organizations, under-control is inefficient because it fails to achieve organizational objectives but nevertheless consumes resources (Bozeman 2000, 95; Landau and Stout 1979). Under-control sometimes signifies ceremonial compliance and legitimacy but is relegated to the organizational outskirts in order to prevent inspection that might reveal its superficial nature (Meyer and Rowan 1977). Ceremonial legitimacy can spill over to individual members, who develop a basis for viewing the organization with suspicion and distrust. Rule behavior is affected as well: superficial compliance is viewed as normless and alienating, with deviance as the response (Barakat 1969).

At the other end of the rule continuum lies over-control, which is a catalyst for red tape (Bozeman 1993, 2000; Bozeman and Feeney 2011). Over-control imposes more constraint than necessary for achieving rule objectives and has consequences for the organization and the individual.[3] From the organizational perspective, over-control is inefficient and requires more constraint than necessary for achieving rule objectives. From the individual perspective, over-control conveys a lack of faith in the capacity of employees to act effectively, asking them to "check their brains at the door" (Adler and Borys 1996, 83). Over-control also sends the message that the organization expects untrustworthy behavior, which in turn can encourage rule violation as a means of individual empowerment and rebellion. This "paradox of formalization" (Sitkin and Bies 1994, 30) has been construed as a "hidden cost" of control that lowers motivation and performance (Falk and Kosfeld 2004; Frey 1993).

Between the extremes of under-control and over-control lies optimal control, which green tape argues is a necessary condition for effective rules. From the organizational perspective, optimal control promises efficiency, signals sincerity in achieving rule purposes, and tells employees and other rule followers that they are trusted enough to not be micromanaged. From the behavioral perspective, optimal control has the greatest chance of evoking rule compliance because it encourages employees to meet the truster's expectations by behaving in trustworthy ways (Bacharach, Guerra, and Zizzo 2001; Braithwaite and Makkai 1994; Guerra and Zizzo 2004; Pettit 1995). In a related strand of research, Lars Tummers, Victor Bekkers, and colleagues found that Dutch mental healthcare professionals who perceived having greater discretion in a new patient reimbursement policy were more willing to cooperate in its implementation (Tummers et al. 2015). Optimal control appears to not only encourage rule compliance; it forgoes the rule rigidity that can accompany excessively controlling environments and discourages the rule-breaking that can accompany inadequate or excessive control.

Given that rules tend to be associated with managerial control, how much over- or under-control tends to be present within an organization's rules? To answer this question, consider a Local Government Workplaces Study survey of individual rules that were collected from a county health department and attendees of an effective rules workshop in 2009. The survey asked the 202 research participants to identify and describe two workplace rules: one they considered

effective and one they considered ineffective. Participants were asked to characterize the effective or ineffective rule on two continuums: between (1) "just the
right amount of control" and "too much control"; and (2) "just the right amount
of control" and "too little control." The survey was distributed at the beginning of
the workshop to avoid bias that might be triggered from anchoring participants
in discussions of rule effectiveness.

The results of the surveys indicate that effective rules tend to be optimally
controlling (see Figure 5.3). Ineffective rules, by contrast, are more likely to be
both under-controlling and over-controlling and least likely to be optimally controlling. Strikingly, under-control is more prevalent among ineffective rules than
over-control in the workshop surveys. This result, based on a limited sample that
is anecdotal at best, suggests that our automatic association of rules with over-
control may be a stereotype that contradicts reality.

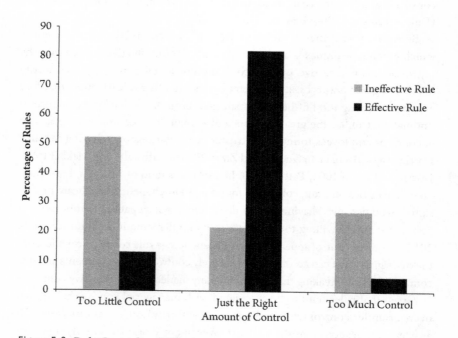

Figure 5.3 Rule Control and Effectiveness
Source: Local Government Workplaces Study, Green Tape Workshops and Organization 5 (n=202).
Workshop participants and health department employees identified one effective and one ineffective
organizational rule and rated each on a range of characteristics, including the extent of overcontrol and
undercontrol.

The idea of optimal rule control raises the question of how one identifies optimality. The quest for optimal control can be likened to a Miles's law dilemma, in which "where you stand depends on where you sit," and the process for finding optimality may be as straightforward as anticipating the consequences of control and simply deciding if they are acceptable. One city manager did so by refusing to install time clocks for hourly employees because he believed that such an action would communicate distrust. The idea here is not to perfectly predict optimal levels of control but rather to engage in practical reasoning to avoid inefficiency and the negative social or psychological consequences of excessive or inadequate control.

Understood Rule Purposes

Rule stakeholders need to understand the *why* of compliance in order for a rule to be effective green tape. As Los Angeles Police Chief Charlie Beck once explained to his officers, "Perceptions matter. It is not enough that you follow the law, you must also confidently explain the reasons you took police action to the people with whom you interact. . . . The act of an unsolicited explanation has tremendous value for everyone involved and goes a long way."[4]

What underlies the power of why? Scholarship on workplace alienation provides a clue. Alienation is a psychological state in which people feel disconnected from work (Kanungo 1979) and work lacks intrinsic meaning for them (Seeman 1959). Work loses meaningfulness when divisions of labor get so complex that employees cannot see their contribution to the "larger logic of production processes" (Erikson 1986). Required activities become meaningless and employees respond by emotionally distancing themselves from the work. On the flip side of the equation, employees who are psychologically connected to the organization are able to locate themselves firmly within its mission. Work is purposeful and easier (Hummel 1994, 111), transparent procedures are enabling (Adler and Borys 1996), and rules are more readily followed (Brown 1974).

Employees interviewed for the LGWS frequently discussed rule purposes, particularly when sharing their thoughts on good rules. Perhaps the most poignant example came from a custodian in a midwestern college town, who commented:

> My department requires us to wear clean uniforms. I'm a dirty worker, so this means I'm not as comfortable as I could be. But I understand: I have to think about how I'm perceived to [*sic*] the public, to the taxpayers who fund us.

The clean uniform rule makes the custodian feel less comfortable. He offsets his discomfort by focusing on the rule's purpose of conveying a professional image to residents. His understanding of the purpose of the rule makes compliance seem less burdensome and more acceptable.

The idea that understanding a rule's purpose facilitates compliance is echoed by the public works secretary who felt she could adhere more fully to rules because she took time to understand them; by the fire department administrative coordinator for whom travel reimbursement forms seemed stupid until she saw the bigger picture; and by the building inspector who felt he could do a better job of explaining to citizens codes that he understood.

One final piece of evidence regarding rule understanding and green tape: Figure 5.4 depicts survey data from Organizations 8 and 9 of the LGWS. The data follows a linear trend: the more workplace rules are perceived as having clear purposes, the more those rules are also perceived as being followed or effective. The practical implication for public managers is to invest time in explaining the purpose of any rule. It will pay off in cooperative rule behavior and, ultimately, a more effective organization.

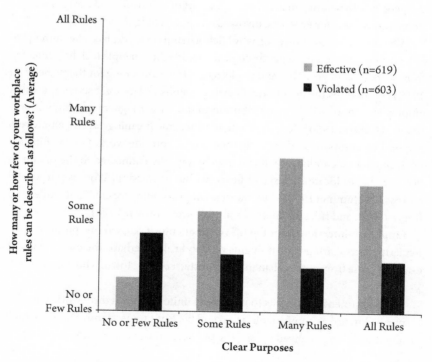

Figure 5.4 Rule Understanding, Effectiveness, and Violation
Source: Local Government Workplaces Study, Organizations 8 and 9, n=603.

Promises and Pitfalls of Green Tape

Green tape theory makes the assumption, first and foremost, that effective organizations require effective rules. Rules are so embedded in the DNA of public organizations that they become a necessary (albeit insufficient) condition for organizational effectiveness. Green tape argues that effective rules require good rules that people will follow. Five attributes of rule design and implementation are expected to achieve rule effectiveness: *rule formalization, rule logic, consistent application, optimal control,* and *understood purpose.* Rule formalization improves rule design, empowers implementation, and facilitates compliance. Rule logic yields a valid means-ends relationship and provides the theoretical "blueprint" that increases the effective pursuit of rule objectives. Optimal control enables the efficient pursuit of rule objectives while communicating organizational trust and value, both of which increase stakeholder cooperation. Consistent rule application—by not systematically exempting particular groups or individuals—is procedurally fair and increases cooperation. And rules with understood purposes make compliance more meaningful and thus more likely to occur.

Each green tape element is necessary but alone is insufficient in creating rule effectiveness. Written rules are legitimizing, but if they are illogically designed they will not achieve rule objectives. Logical rules are more likely to achieve objectives but less likely to do so if stakeholders do not understand their purpose. Rules that are consistently applied but overly controlling may appear fair to stakeholders, but a concomitant appearance of managerial distrust may undermine cooperation. Stakeholders may understand a rule's purpose, but if the rule's logic is not sound, they may not cooperate. Effective rules require the simultaneous presence of all five green tape attributes.

Green tape theory makes several contributions to the scholarship on organizational rules. By focusing on effective rules, green tape expands current scholarly thinking beyond red tape concerns and creates a more comprehensive view of rules than currently exists in the public management literature. A positive rules approach also holds promise for strengthening the relevance of public management scholarship to managers, a plus for any applied field. Second, green tape is based on a range of hierarchical perspectives: the perspective of organizational elites is important but so are the voices of sanitation workers, health department nurses, building inspectors, and public works secretaries. This variety and expression of lived experiences strengthens the empirical base upon which green tape theory is built. A third advantage is that green tape provides a theory-based practical guide for creating effective organizational rules. The theory is grounded but also connected to research from a range of disciplines to back up its arguments.

But there are chinks in the green tape armor, chief among them the assumption

Figure 5.5   Green Tape Attributes

that rules emerge from prosocial motives. This assumption is rendered problematic by a world with villains. Public administration scholars Guy Adams and Danny Balfour note that rules can be an instrument of evil, as illustrated by the interrogation policies that allowed torture and abuse to occur at Abu Ghraib prison in Iraq (2009). In sharp contrast, green tape was crafted with the benevolent public administrator in mind, paring down the world to a subset of reality. A second chink pertains to the micro nature of green tape and the specific conditions under which rules are theoretically made effective. Less attention is paid to the macro role of effective rules in society; it is simply assumed. On the upside, the absence of a macro view related to green tape is an opportunity for future research. A final chink relates to the viewpoint assumed by the research. Green tape is based on a diversity of employee perspectives but is written for the public manager. Other lenses through which to view the public organization—the citizen's, the immigrant's, the regulated's, to name just a few—might produce a different conception of effective organizational rules.

Green Tape and the Five-Second Rule

To illustrate a green tape failure, consider the fate of the "Five-Second Rule," an informal crowd control policy of Missouri police suspended by a federal judge in October 2014 (Abdullah vs. County of St. Louis). The setting is Ferguson, Missouri, where citizens have been gathering to protest a fatal police shooting. Most of the citizen gatherings are peaceful but a few turn violent. A Quik Trip convenience store is vandalized and burned to the ground. Molotov cocktails are thrown. A member of the crowd is beaten unconscious. Governor Jay Nixon calls a state of emergency and forms a unified command structure with the St. Louis County police and the Missouri Highway Patrol.

The command post is set up a mile from the main protests and members of the crowd shout plans to overrun it. In response, the officers devise a Five-Second Rule as unwritten policy for controlling the crowds. The rule prohibits gatherers from stopping on the sidewalks for more than five seconds; any length beyond that makes them subject to arrest or threat of arrest. The rule is announced at roll calls, where officers are told to use their discretion but given no written guidelines for when or how the rule should be used. Thus the first attribute of green tape—rule formalization—is not met.

Recall that rule formalization is both a process and an outcome. As a process, it imposes on rule design the discipline and transparency of writing. As an outcome, rule formalization conveys the legitimacy of a rule's authority. By virtue of its unwritten status, the Five-Second Rule was not carefully designed, vetted by stakeholders, or legitimate, all of which are key benefits of rule formalization. Clues about these failures emerge from confusion over the authoritative origins of the rule (which was erroneously ascribed to Missouri's failure-to-disperse laws[5]); the verbal explanations that instructed officers to "use their discretion"[6]; and the creation of a rule that did not consider all stakeholder perspectives, including the rule's constitutionality.

The Five-Second Rule also failed the second green tape criterion of logical design. The rule sought crowd control, a legitimate police objective affirmed by Judge Perry. But the rule's underlying theory—that moving gatherers along would reduce violence and increase the ability of police to manage the crowd—was flawed. Judge Perry noted the absence of reasoning or evidence from the police that the five-second rule was an effective crowd-control tactic, observing that, "In fact, one of the police witnesses testified that it only worked well during the daytime when there were no large crowds and no threats of violence—when the crowds grew unruly, telling them to keep moving was not an effective strategy."

The Five-Second Rule was also inconsistently applied, representing its third green tape failure. Inconsistent application is the death knell for any rule, as it undercuts a rule's purpose and creates procedural injustice among rule-followers. As the injunction describes, some officers enforced the rule but others did not. Some reporters were subjected to the rule, others were not. Slowly moving gatherers were told to speed it up; small groups of people were threatened with arrest if they did not keep moving. The Five-Second Rule not only failed to control the crowds, it evoked such a strong sense of procedural injustice that it triggered a federal lawsuit.

The Five-Second Rule also violated the green tape criterion of optimal control by imposing constraint not only excessive but unconstitutional. Unconstitutionality, a rare but poignant test of rule control, is relevant to a range of public organizational rules, including protected speech, drug testing, and due process. If a public organizational rule violates a citizen's or employee's constitutional rights, by definition it imposes more control than necessary.[7] The excessive control imposed by the Five-Second Rule proved organizationally inefficient and procedurally unjust to the citizens involved (and landed St. Louis County and the Missouri Highway Patrol in court), and it was counterproductive to the behaviors it evoked (rule-bending and rule-rigidity in equal measure and a lawsuit to boot).

Finally, the Five-Second Rule violated the green tape criterion of having an understood rule purpose, as was evident through only sporadic awareness of the rule's existence throughout the police hierarchy. The *Washington Post* quoted the St. Louis County police chief as saying, "I've never heard of such a rule," and the ranking Missouri Highway Patrol officer claimed no knowledge of the rule until the lawsuit.[8] Along with lumpy awareness of the rule's existence, the meanings attached to the rule varied widely, as the injunction indicates:

> These witnesses' testimony was inconsistent, however, about what the strategy meant and how it was to be enforced. The St. Louis County Police Chief testified that the strategy was only intended to be used when crowds became dangerously large and unruly, which had mostly happened in the nighttime. The Chief testified that he had been instructed to use "failure to disperse" to enforce the strategy. He also testified that now that the Ferguson Police Department is the law enforcement agency in charge of the area, the St. Louis County police will not be using the keep-moving strategy. His subordinate, however, who was responsible for communicating the strategy to the officers in the field, testified to no such limitations. Instead he said officers were just told to use their discretion. He testified that the strategy could be used at any time, and did not require a riot or unlawful assembly. He also testified that the strategy was still in effect and that he would use it again if sent back to

Ferguson. The Highway Patrol Field Operations Commander (the second highest-ranking officer in the Highway Patrol) testified that because the legal authority for the keep-moving strategy was the failure-to-disperse law, people who refused to keep moving could only be arrested if the elements of that law were met.

The injunction portrays an unclear rule that was widely misunderstood. The circumstances triggering the rule, its authoritative origins, and its institutional applicability were murky at best. Without shared organizational understanding of the Five-Second Rule's means and ends, the rule lacked the cognitive power to qualify as green tape.

The Five-Second Rule illustrates the interdependent nature of the five green tape attributes. The unwritten quality of the Five-Second Rule led to its illogical and overly controlling design, which in turn yielded to inconsistent and misunderstood implementation. The Five-Second Rule represents a total green tape failure, although one that was predictable under the circumstances. As the chapter on rule behavior discusses, high-pressure situations such as Ferguson are not conducive to well-formulated rules because they reduce the time available to think through problems and solutions.

It is important to note that the Five-Second Rule cannot be characterized as red tape because red tape is defined as ineffective *written* rules, as opposed to Ferguson's unwritten five-second policy. Furthermore, the green tape attributes of rule formalization, consistency, and understood purposes point to flaws of the Five-Second Rule that red tape theory could not have captured. A further comparison of red and green tape theories for their conceptual similarities and differences will be useful and help find opportunities to entwine the concepts in future research.

Red Tape vs. Green Tape

Public organizations are stereotyped for being purveyors of bad rules. A *Washington Post* cartoon from 2009 depicts dozens of tangled stoplights suspended over a street. Interspersed among the stoplights are signs that read "Rules of the Road," "Wall Street," and "One Way." Two men in hardhats look up at the stoplights. One comments, "What we need here is more rules." A lighted billboard to their left reads: "Big Government at Work."

The cartoon speaks volumes to how American society perceives public sector rules: voluminous, ineffective, excessively restrictive, and self-perpetuating. No doubt these adjectives accurately describe some public sector rules. But the

Local Government Workplaces Study portrays a more nuanced picture. Figure 5.6 depicts the distribution of survey responses from employees of eight organizations, on a scale from ineffective to effective. Roughly one in five respondents place rules on the ineffective (left-handed) side of the scale, 40 percent perceive rules as mostly effective (the right-hand side of the scale), and not quite 40 percent see a mix of good and bad rules in their workplaces (the middle of the scale). These results are a far cry from the image of public organizations as bureaucratically entangled.

Given the importance of rules to effective public sector functioning, it is perhaps surprising that only two theories of public management address the precursors to effective rules: red tape and green tape. Red tape emerged as a public management research topic in the 1990s, when public management scholar Barry Bozeman formalized his observations of ineffective rules in the New York State Energy Research and Development Authority. Based on this rule-complex organization, Bozeman identified two types of red tape: rule-inception and rule-evolved. Rule-inception red tape entails "rules born bad," that is, arising from

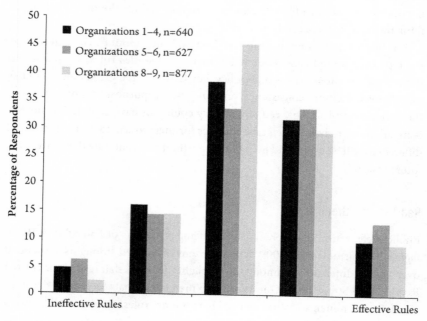

Figure 5.6 Rule Effectiveness in Local Government Organizations
Source: Local Government Workplaces Study. Based on two types of questions: where workplace rules fall between opposite characteristics (ineffective to effective); and the extent of effective rules (from no rules to all rules).

sources such as flawed behavioral forecasts, illegitimate managerial purposes, and political or managerial over-control. Rule-evolved red tape involves rules that go bad and become irrelevant over time, due to flawed implementation or shifting circumstances. Out of this research Bozeman also developed the first measurable definition of red tape as the rules, regulations, and procedures that remain in place and entail a compliance burden but serve no legitimate purpose (1993).

Since Bozeman's first work on red tape, an international community of public management scholars has emerged to produce more than fifty articles on an array of red tape effects (Bozeman and Feeney 2011, 13), including managerial alienation (DeHart-Davis and Pandey 2005); role ambiguity (Pandey and Rainey 2006); and organizational performance (Brewer and Walker 2010; Pandey and Moynihan 2005; Walker and Brewer 2008). While the subject of red tape has a rich and burgeoning literature, it is not without limitations. As Bozeman and Feeney note in their embedded criticism of the concept (2011), the majority of red tape studies derive from a small number of datasets; their foundational data tends to favor managers over frontline workers; they employ perceptual survey measures that arguably do not tap red tape; and much of the original theory (rule-evolved vs. rule-inception) has not been tested (Bozeman and Feeney 2011). Yet this scholarship's importance cannot be understated: it is one of the few research topics in public management than can claim to be homegrown and free of umbilical ties to sociology, political science, or economics.

Green tape theory, a newcomer to the theoretical landscape, shares similarities with red tape. Both red tape and green tape emerged from qualitative research, specifically interview data (state agency employees for red tape, local government employees for green tape). Rule effectiveness is the explanatory phenomenon of interest to both red tape and green tape. Both concepts use rule control, design logic, and compliance as explanatory variables. Control in red tape terms stems from political overreaction and managerial micromanagement; control in green tape is managerial and resides on a continuum between inadequate and excessive constraint. The logic of rule design figures into red tape and green tape in apposite fashion, with the extent of rule logic strengthening or undercutting rule effectiveness. Regarding compliance, red tape is defined by written rules that remain in place and entail a compliance burden (Bozeman 2000), which implies that without compliance there is no red tape. Similarly, green tape requires (in addition to well-designed rules) the cooperation of rule stakeholders, or those who enforce, explain, and comply with rules (DeHart-Davis 2009a). Without compliance, both colors of tape are nonexistent.

But two significant differences between the red tape and green tape theories blur the appearance of mirror image concepts. A primary distinction lies in rule formalization, that is, the written quality of the organization's rule. Red tape is defined by ineffective written rules; by comparison rule formalization—the extent to which a rule is specified in writing—is variable in the green tape framework. Rules can be higher or lower in rule formalization, the variance of which is expected to contribute significantly to organizational effectiveness. Thus red tape holds rule formalization constant, while green tape allows it to vary.

A second distinction lies in the scope of explanations posed. Red tape theory casts a wide theoretical net to predict bad rules. Red tape explanatory factors range from broad macro-level forces like shifting rule ecologies, conflicting public policy objectives, entropy, and ownership, to micro-level influences such as self-aggrandizement, alienation, and risk aversion. By contrast, green tape is narrower in scope and focused on attributes of rule design and implementation that raise or lower rule effectiveness. Green tape is, in many ways, a stakeholder theory of organizational rules that accords a starring role to those who explain, enforce, and comply. Because people experience and respond to rules in manifold ways, rules must be technically sound and socially acceptable to work well. Red tape theory incorporates some types of individual behavior but largely casts ineffective burdensome rules as a system problem rather than a people problem (Bozeman 2000, 38).

Is red tape truly a systems problem rather than a people problem? Looking at correlations from survey data in the LGWS (Table 5.1), employees do not associate red tape with written rules. By contrast, red tape strongly correlates with centralization, or the need to secure verbal permission from above to address small issues. If red tape has less to do with written rules and more to do with personalized authority, then red tape is a people problem rather than a systems problem. This is good news for public managers because it suggests that red tape is solvable: authority can be decentralized and hierarchical layers can be reduced. By contrast, if red tape is a systems problem, it poses the more difficult prospect of tackling an impenetrable foe. Red tape as a people problem gives hope.

Public organizations invariably have both red and green tape, but can a rule be both at one time? The answer is yes. Consider there are three types of red tape: stakeholder, organizational, and multidimensional (Bozeman and Feeney 2011, 44). Stakeholder red tape resides in the eye of the beholder and represents rules that do not benefit stakeholder objectives. Organizational red tape is construed from the perspective of the organization and involves rules that consume resources yet fail to achieve predetermined objectives. Multidimensional red tape involves rules that are ineffective from either the perspective of the organization or its stakeholders. This approach loosens Bozeman's original definition of

Table 5.1 Red Tape, Rule Formalization, and Centralization

	Organizations 1–4			Organizations 6–7		
	Red Tape	Rule Formalization	Centralization	Red Tape	Rule Formalization	Centralization
Red Tape						
Pearson Correlation	1	−0.02	.26*	1	−0.11	.30*
Sig. (2-tailed)	0	0.65	0		0.001	0
N	640	630	630	847	828	829
Rule Formalization						
Pearson Correlation	−0.02	1	−0.06	−0.11	1	−0.14
Sig. (2-tailed)	0.65	0	0.13	0.001		0
N	630	633	626	828	1,467	1,408
Centralization						
Pearson Correlation	.26*	−0.06	1	.30*	−0.14	1
Sig. (2-tailed)	0	0.13	0	0	0	
N	630	626	635	829	1,408	1,455

*Correlation is significant at the 0.01 level (2-tailed).

red tape as rules having no redeeming social value, which has proved to be a strict standard to which few rules adhere. The definition also makes room for both subjective and objective assessments of red tape, which is helpful given that red tape is an inherently social construct that is difficult to diagnose apart from the humans who perceive it (2011, 35).

In contrast, green tape theory accords stakeholders a significant causal role in rule effectiveness even though the theoretical end game is still the achievement of organizational purposes (DeHart-Davis 2009a). Thus, a rule in itself can be green tape if it achieves organizational purposes but identified as stakeholder red tape if it burdens a particular group without benefit. For example, a grievance policy that seeks to reduce employee complaints by imposing short filing deadlines could be considered green tape (achieving organizational purposes) but stakeholder red tape (imposing a burden on employees that yields them no benefit). Similarly, partially effective rules could qualify as multidimensional red tape vis-à-vis some organizational objectives but green tape on other organizational objectives.

Inevitably, public organizations have both red tape and green tape: some rules work, others fail, and a few do a little of both. At this point in time, public management research has yet to tackle these situations of mixed red and green tape. This line of inquiry could explore within public organizations the distribution of "tape ratios," the determinants of those ratios, and the influence of different tape ratios on organizational effectiveness. These possibilities are contemplated in the next chapter. In the meantime, red tape and green tape are useful concepts for guiding both public management research and practical efforts at designing and implementing effective organizational rules.

Summary

Public organizations seeking to create effective rules must consider a range of issues. The first is whether a written rule is truly needed. Organizational scholarship and conventional wisdom suggest that rules are ideally written in response to persistent organizational problems with reasonably well-understood causes. Once the decision to write a written rule is made, stakeholders should be involved in rule design as all three perspectives of the organizational rules framework come into play. Organizational purposes must be identified, along with the human interactions that ultimately elicit voluntary rather than coerced cooperation. These considerations inform an expanded conceptualization of rule effectiveness, that is more empowering and less controlling than ones operating in public organizations of yesteryear.

The green tape theory of rules provides guidance on the characteristics that make or break rule effectiveness. Defined as good rules that people will follow, green tape is most likely to arise from rules that are written, logical, consistently applied, optimally controlling, and understood. These attributes contribute to rule effectiveness by furthering organizational objectives and structuring person-organization interactions that motivate voluntary cooperation rather than resistance. An analysis of an unwritten crowd control policy used by Missouri police demonstrates a failed rule that does not count as red tape but flunks the green tape test by missing all the elements of an effective rule. A side-by-side comparison of red and green tape theories suggests that future research could fuse these concepts and derive a more complete understanding of organization rule effectiveness. A step in that direction has been suggested by public management scholar Erin Borry, who devised a new measure of red tape using green tape survey items (2016).

Effective rules require time, attention, and focused managerial action. Given the precarious economic and political environment in which public organizations currently reside, effective public organizations need effective rules, whether to achieve accountability, demonstrate legitimacy, or safeguard employee morale. Simply put, public organizations cannot afford to have bad rules.

Notes

1. For more on logic as the hallmark of rational thinking, see Hummel 2008, 35; Thompson 1967, 85; Stinchcombe 2001; Hasselbladh and Kallinikos 2000; Landau and Stout 1979.

2. It is also possible that the training of ticket agents to detect lies somehow failed. This counterargument assumes that lie detection is reliable, valid, and can be communicated through training. Returning to the conditions for rule-writing: it is not clear that the technology exists to detect lies from airline terrorists (Vrij 2008).

3. A prime suspect in overcontrol is legalism: organizations create rules that mimic legal structures in an attempt to achieve legitimacy and lower legal risk. The grievance policies discussed in the last chapter are good examples of this phenomenon. By plopping templates derived from law onto organizational settings where they may not fit, organizations can impose constraints beyond those needed to achieve internal organizational purposes.

4. See Beck's message of January 2011 at http://lapdblog.typepad.com/lapd_blog/2011/01/january-2011-chiefs-message.html.

5. The court injunction (Mo. Rev. Stat. § 574.060, entitled "Refusal to disperse") states that a "person commits the crime of refusal to disperse if, being present at the scene of an unlawful assembly, or at the scene of a riot, he knowingly fails or refuses to obey the lawful command of a law enforcement officer to depart from the scene of such unlawful assembly or riot." An "unlawful assembly" requires that six or more people assemble and agree to violate laws with force or violence (Mo. Rev. Stat. § 574.040).

6. Abdullah v. County of St. Louis, Missouri, United States District Court, E.D. Missouri, Eastern Division 2014.

7. From the injunction: "Thus, defendants' own evidence shows that this strategy fails the requirement that 'the means chosen are not substantially broader than necessary to achieve the government's interest.'" Ward v. Rock Against Racism, 491 U.S. 781, 7989-9 (1989).

8. "Federal Judges Tosses '5 Second Rule' Being Used to Police Ferguson Protests," *Washington Post*, October 6, 2014.

CONCLUSION

Rules are indispensable to public organization functioning, although they are not understood as such. Rules assume a variety of forms—as standard operating procedures, as policy manuals, as operational guidelines—and they accomplish a staggering array of managerial tasks: they manage human capital, control public finances, and provide structure for interactions with citizens, to name just a few. Indeed, there is *zero* evidence that public organizations of any substantial size can function without rules. Yet scholars and practitioners alike tend to focus on the negative consequences of rules, whether that is red tape, inefficiency, rigidity, or organizational sluggishness. This distorted view of rules yields a lopsided and biased portrait of reality that limits understanding of this most basic form of organizational structure.

Our discussion concludes with a consideration of the possibilities for future organizational rules research by public management scholars. The chapter highlights key points of the organizational rules framework and reflects on the multiplicity of academic disciplines contributing to it. It identifies opportunities for future organizational research that is engaged, citizen-focused, and policy relevant. A different thinking about organizational rules is suggested, one that holds implications for public management practice, research, and teaching of the future.

The Organizational Rules Framework Revisited

The organizational rules framework features three perspectives: the organizational, the individual, and the behavioral. Each perspective assumes a different vantage point for understanding organizational rules and is grounded in evidence from the Local Government Workplaces Study as well as in diverse intellectual trains of thought.

The organizational perspective (outlined in chapter 1) focuses on rule

functions. Carved from organizational theory and the insights of local government managers, this perspective views rules as one way that organizations
adapt to their environment to ensure their continued survival. The written word
empowers the capacity of the organizational rules to communicate across time
and space, to order time, and to accumulate knowledge. Rules shift authority
from the individual to the group and allow collective goals to be pursued. Within
the broad category of rational action, rules serve discrete purposes: to coordinate, constrain, and empower; to convey behavioral expectations and socialize
to organizational norms and values; to create, store, and disseminate knowledge; and to secure legitimacy. (See Table C.1 for a general explanation of these
multiple purposes and how they are accomplished.) While not always perfectly
successful in achieving these goals, rules are indisputably necessary for enabling
rational action within public organizations.

   The individual perspective (examined in chapter 2) explains how employees experience an organization's rules. This perspective is guided by theory
from sociology and social psychology as well as the employees who shared
their rule experiences during the Local Government Workplaces Study. Even
when employees do not directly experience a rule, they observe how the rule is
designed and implemented and draw conclusions about the nature of the organization and its regard for employees (Table C.2). Through these different experiences, rules structure the relationship between employee and organization.

   The behavioral perspective (addressed in chapter 3) shifts attention to actions

Table C.1 The Organizational Perspective: Key Findings

Rule Function	Local Government Workplace Project Findings
Organizational Rationality	Rules associate with higher mission effectiveness.
Coordination	Rules associate with stronger teamwork.
Constraint and Empowerment	Survey participants construe rules as more helpful than harmful.
Conveys Behavioral Expectations	Survey participants with more workplace rules also perceive greater clarity in their roles.
Socialization	Survey participants in workplaces with more organizational rules are more likely to see organizational values play out in the workplace.
Knowledge and Learning	Written rules are perceived as more logical than unwritten rules.
Legitimacy	Rules demonstrate the organization's acceptability and worthiness to the outside world.

taken in response to rules (Table C.3). A diverse body of scholarship informs the behavioral perspective, from the work of economists and political scientists to students of social work and street-level bureaucracy. Within this perspective, rules are interpreted and enforced and followed or violated, all with more or less discretion. Shades of behavioral gray reside within each of these categories, making rule behavior highly varied and complex.

The behavioral perspective also identifies organizational and individual influences on rule behavior, as well as points of convergence between the two (see Table C.4). Public managers can manipulate some of these influences, whether rule characteristics or performance pressures. Other influences, such as

Table C.2 The Individual Perspective: Key Findings

Rule Experiences	Findings
Empowerment and Constraint	Rules empower and constrain individual behavior. Survey participants in organizations with more written rules report a higher sense of authorization.
Legitimacy	Rules legitimize organizational directives and make them appear authoritative, neutral, and worthy of cooperation. Rule legitimacy is associated with higher compliance.
Procedural Fairness	Rules convey fairness when designed with employee input and administered consistently. Employees involved in rule design perceive rules as more effective than those in whose design they are not involved. Rule consistency and employee input both correlate with perceptions of fair rules, but consistency bears a stronger correlation.
Social Leveling	Rules put employees of different social strata on more equal footing. Women report positive attitudes toward rule abidance and more favorable perceptions of rules than their male counterparts. Employees with greater commitment to unions perceive less red tape.
Trust	Rules convey messages of both trust and distrust between managers and employees. Burdensome rules correlate with perceived supervisory distrust. Inconsistently applied rules are associated with lower trust in upper management. Written rules correlate with perceptions of truthfulness and benevolence.
Organizational Identification	Rules create shared meaning and a framework for viewing contributions to the organization. Survey participants with more rules in their workplaces also identify more strongly with their organizations.

Table C.3 The Behavioral Perspective: Organizational Rule Behaviors

Rule Behavior	Findings
Interpretation	Rule interpretation translates a rule's intent and assigns its meaning to the situation at hand.
Compliance	Organizational rules are mostly followed. Compliance can be normal, rigid, malicious, or excessive. Eighty-five percent of survey participants report that no or few rules are violated; not quite a third indicate some rules are violated.
Violation	Rules can be bent (complied with only partially) or broken (willfully disregarded). A variety of motivations drive rule violation. Survey participants most likely to agree that they will bend rules for prosocial motivations are least likely to agree that they will bend rules to make their jobs easier.
Discretion	Discretionary rule behaviors arise from employees' ability to make decisions about rules without consulting organizational authority. When rules are incomplete, vaguely worded, or conflict with other rules, discretion can be organizationally deliberate (built into rules) or unintentional.
Enforcement	Enforcers interpret rules and decide whether and how to apply them. They explain rules to followers, monitor compliance, and deliver noncompliance consequences. Sixty-three percent of survey participants disagree that they are being watched to see if they follow rules.

personality and gender socialization, are beyond organizational reach. The sweep of rule behaviors and influences portrays public employees as active contributors to the reality of organizational rules, as opposed to passive recipients of organizational structure.

Application of the organizational framework to non-union grievance policies in North Carolina local governments (discussed in chapter 4) shows that local governments use grievance policies to manage legal risk, give voice to dissenters, and convey legal legitimacy to the outside world. Grievance policies can convey procedural fairness, trust, and legitimacy, or, conversely, procedural unfairness, distrust and untrustworthiness, and illegitimacy. Grievance policies also send signals about individual standing and worth and reveal to employees the true nature of the organization (especially when grievance processes appear to be rubber stamps for managerial action). The behavioral perspective reveals that managers sometimes avoid rule enforcement or disregard grievance process requirements as a way of preventing grievances. Employees can file nuisance grievances and comply maliciously; for example, they might share minimal information during investigative fact-finding as a form of protest. Thinking about grievance policies

Table C.4 The Behavioral Perspective: Influences on Rule Behavior

Rule Behavior	Conclusions
Personality	Bureaucratic personalities are faithful rule-followers; unbureaucratic personalities view rules as optional constraints on discretion; average rule personalities respect rules but will question them when needed.
Organizational Power	Rule behavior can serve as a source of three types of power: compensatory (overcoming a lack of standing), maintenance (retaining or expanding sources of personal influence), or interpersonal (between two or more organizational members).
Socialization	Rule behavior is a function of socialization: from peers, by professionalization, due to gender, or via the organizational culture.
Risks and Benefits	Employees calculate the risks and benefits of compliance vs. violation in deciding on rule behavior.
Legitimacy	The appearance of neutral authority in organizational rules (driven particularly by their written quality) increases legitimacy and encourages compliance.
Performance Pressures	When time is short and expectations are high, rule violations are more likely to occur.
Faulty Rules	Rules that are illogically designed, overly detailed, conflicting, voluminous, rapidly changing, or burdensome are more likely to be violated. Rules perceived as red tape (because they are burdensome and ineffective) are associated with more favorable attitudes toward rule-bending.
Judgment	Employees apply personal judgment in deciding on rule behavior: experiential (prior experience, on-the-job training, trial and error); moral (personal sense of right and wrong); or situational (whether to follow or violate based on characteristics of the situation at hand).

from these alternative vantage points enables a more comprehensive understanding than could be gleaned from any single perspective alone.

All three perspectives provide theory-based practical guidance for creating effective organizational rules (chapter 5). Each prescriptive element is based on the organizational, individual, and behavioral perspective on rules. Effective rules should be conceptualized not only as a way to achieve organizational purposes but as a vehicle for getting voluntary cooperation and creating positive interactions between employees and organizations. Rules should be written only when there are significant organizational problems and reasonably clear solutions to those problems. Stakeholders should be consulted in rule design, not only to secure cooperation and convey procedural fairness but also to overcome flaws that are commonly created when rule designers and rule users are different organizational folk. Green tape theory is used to identify five attributes for guiding effective organization rule design and implementation: rule formalization, rule logic, consistent application, optimal control, and rule understanding. The "Five-Second Rule," a failed crowd-control policy of Missouri police, illustrates an organization rule failure; all green tape attributes were missing and the rule was overturned in federal court. Comparing red tape to green tape, both theories emphasize distinct concepts that together could provide a more holistic approach to rule effectiveness in public organizations.

Beyond the organizational rules framework, the research collected by the Local Government Workplaces Study yielded findings that were surprising and sometimes contradictory to organizational rules scholarship. For example, "red tape" was rarely referenced in interviews with local government employees. Despite the term's use in everyday language and its enduring association with public organizations, only a handful of local government employees used it in their comments (and sometimes in ways inconsistent with its scholarly definition). The most common frustration with rules was not excessive control or administrative burden but rather inconsistent rule application. Rules were generally viewed in a positive light, with an intuitive understanding of all three perspectives of the organizational rules framework. Even when participating employees disagreed with or were inconvenienced by a given rule, they displayed a keen awareness of its purpose(s).

Future Avenues for Organizational Rules Research

The organizational rules framework takes an analytical eclecticism approach, which is drawn on different intellectual traditions to shed light on a subject matter (Raadschelders 2011, 191). Thus, no single academic discipline has intellectual market share. To contingency theorists, rules align the organization with its environment, manage complexity, and ensure survival. Political scientists and economists harness self-interest to explain rule behavior. Sociologists identify organizational variations in rules and examine their effects on organization members. Social psychologists bring legitimacy, procedural fairness, and social identity to the table. Last, but not least, public management scholars breathe contextual life into the study of organizational rules and demonstrate the ill effects of bad rules. Understanding the beneficial and harmful aspects of organizational rules requires a broad theoretical net.

Along with its multidisciplinary foundation, knowledge of rules benefits from a diversity of methods. In the qualitative tradition, researchers have employed ethnography, phenomenology, field research, and grounded theory to shed light on organizational rules, as illuminated by data collected through interviews, participant observation, archival records, case studies, and content and narrative analyses. On the quantitative side, rules researchers analyze original and secondary data through surveys and experiments, and archives and interviews. This mosaic of approaches enables a fuller portrayal of organizational rules than could be achieved by singular methods alone. More broadly, methodological diversity is a prerequisite to the intellectual health of the public administration field, enabling a greater connection between theory and reality (Nesbit et al. 2010; Riccucci 2010).

Engaged scholarship is another form of intellectual pluralism that may provide benefits for organizational rules research. Engaged scholarship connects theory with practice by conducting academic research that contributes to both scholarly and practical concerns. Scholars interested in creating formal knowledge gain access to practical settings and, in turn, provide useful information back to practitioners. Engaged research is both opportunistic and politically savvy, given the pitiful funding sources and increased pressure on academics to demonstrate their usefulness to society. On the practitioner side, public organizations are notoriously cash-strapped and few can afford private consultants to conduct internal research. Conducting engaged scholarship is thus a win-win that promises to improve both public management practice and theory.

Citizens' perspectives on organizational rules provide one such engaged scholarship opportunity. In an era of public management that refers to citizens as "customers" (Fountain 2001), more research is needed on citizen experiences in encountering, interpreting, and following organizational rules. This is not a new idea to public management scholars: Barry Bozeman and Mary Feeney argue that citizen perspectives are essential if red tape scholarship is to flourish (2011, 125); Richard Walker and Gene Brewer (2008) distinguish ineffective rules according to whether they affect employees (internally) or citizens (externally); Lars Tummers and his colleagues find that useless rules lower citizen satisfaction (2015). Applying red tape to democracy rights and responsibilities, Donald Moynihan and Pamela Herd make the case that rules can be used to curtail the full participation of citizens, using voting rights and welfare policy as an example (2010). In a contribution to public management scholarship, sociologist Celeste Watkins-Hayes raises the possibility that red tape (i.e., heavy rules and bureaucratic impersonality combined) is likely to drive a wedge between bureaucrats and clients of the same race, undercutting the notion of representative bureaucracy (2011). Another promising line of inquiry originates in the work of Evelyn Brodkin and Malay Majmundar, who examine the potential for "proceduralism" (including misapplication of rules) to create a class of administratively disadvantaged people (2010). These studies all represent a start to research that links rules to broader themes of citizenship, democracy, and social equity.

Public policy implementation provides another avenue for organizational rules research. Scratching the surface of this topic, a 2015 study by Mads Jakobsen and Peter Mortensen finds that an increase in Danish laws mandating performance management in school systems coincides with the creation of organizational rules for performance management (as measured by executive orders). This finding should be no surprise: without organizational rules there is no way to coordinate action, empower and constrain individual actors, or elicit acceptable rule behaviors. Public administration scholar Charles Goodsell makes a similar case for bureaucracy more broadly, using examples from healthcare reform to postal delivery to homeland security (2014). Without bureaucracy, Goodsell argues, these public services are simply not deliverable.

But rules and bureaucracy alone are not enough: as a study of the reform of a welfare-to-work program in California demonstrates, even when rules were in place and technically followed, social workers lacked the training, information, and evidence of policymaker commitment needed to effectively implement change (Meyer, Glaser, and MacDonald 1998). Organizational rules are one link from policy formulation to implementation (Crosby 1996; Sandfort and Moulton 2015) that could use greater scholarly attention, whether to explain environmental regulation, social welfare reform, or public health initiatives.

Thinking Differently about Rules

The organizational rules framework suggests a shift in thinking about rules: from constraint to capacity, from direction to interaction, from control to influence. How could this shift alter how rules are enacted within public organizations? Only time will tell, but a few ideas come to mind. As a beginning, public organizations could post their policies, procedures, and guidelines online, to reflect the values of transparency and accountability. Every rule could be introduced by an authoritative source with its objective clearly stated, based on the realization that employees will more readily cooperate when they know why they should do what they are being asked to do. Because rules empower as well as constrain, public organizational rules could identify areas of employee discretion, along with guiding principles to be considered when making discretionary rule decisions. Rules could be reviewed on a staggered two-year cycle for potential elimination, revision, or maintenance, based on the construction of rules as containers for organizational learning.

To incorporate a diversity of perspectives and enable employee voice, employees in good standing from across the hierarchy could be eligible to serve on policy review and creation committees. Policies could be carefully worded to avoid negative language and employ positive language to aid problem-solving. Because rules would continually be refreshed and carefully crafted, inconsistent rule application would rarely be a problem and thus this source of procedural unfairness would be avoided. Organizational practices such as paternity leave, conflict resolution, and incentive prizes could be incorporated in the quest for innovation and legitimacy. Annual employee surveys could assess the effectiveness of specific rules and training on policies and procedures (e.g., gauging whether they are highly effective, time-efficient, and entertaining), which would be encoded in the organizational DNA.

The organizational rules framework could shift scholarly thinking as well. The most fundamental change would occur in how rules are studied, that is, as ratios of green tape to red tape. Public organizations invariably have both, and "tape" ratios could be identified as one marker of organizational health, predicting organizational outcomes related to innovation, organizational capital, and performance. Rules could be construed as a telling piece of the organization whole and reveal how public organizations situate themselves within their environment, how they treat the people residing within their walls, and the shared values that comprise their organizational culture. Rules could also be measured more carefully, as distinctive elements of organizational design disagglomerated from centralization and hierarchy.

The organizational rules framework could also translate into the classroom. Rather than thinking of rules as management tools of last resort, students could apply the organizational rules framework to the formulation of hypothetical rules and anticipate the individual, behavioral, and organizational consequences. Students would become aware of rules as a kind of "tie that binds" because they structure the relationship between individuals and organizations. Classroom activities could suss out the less obvious aspects of rules to see how employees could be empowered or constrained, to diagnose how organizations could employ rules to symbolize legitimacy, or to anticipate the range of behavioral responses to rules. Students could be taught to diagnose red tape versus green tape, to discern the management philosophies underlying an organization's rules, and to predict the messages that different rules convey.

A shift in thinking about rules promises to yield more expansive rules scholarship and greater public service effectiveness. This is not to say, however, that rules are a panacea for solving public organization problems. Public managers must motivate employees despite tightened resources, higher service expectations, and a vitriolic political climate. Race and gender bias still plague critical aspects of government service delivery, most visibly in policing. With the advent of social media, citizens play a more prominent role in evaluating the performance of public organizations, both fairly or unfairly. Organizational rules are unlikely to solve these thorny issues. Without effective rules to ensure smooth background functioning, the public sector has a diminished capacity to devote to the critical issues of the day.

A Tribute

The city and county employees of the Local Government Workplaces Study have conveyed volumes about the realities of public sector life. They have informed a panoramic view of rules that transcends narrow theoretical conceptions and remote academic musings. City and county employees are not saints. Rather, they are flesh-and-blood human beings who profoundly influence a community's quality of life. Working for the public in the most mundane and profound of ways, local government employees serve citizens who can be hostile and elected officials who sometimes view them as expendable. Yet they persevere, albeit imperfectly, in delivering public goods and services that lay the foundation of citizens' quality of life. Public administration is infinitely knowable through their eyes, and the glimpses they have given here expand our understanding of the most critical and vilified facilitator of government functioning: the organizational rule.

APPENDIX: LOCAL GOVERNMENT WORKPLACES STUDY DESIGN

The Local Government Workplaces Study began in 2004 at the University of Kansas. Local government organizations—roughly one per year—were recruited to participate in a low-cost (often no-cost) employee survey. The original recruitment announcement emphasized organization rules (see Box A.1); over time, recruitment messages shifted to the opportunity for local governments to understand employee morale. Nine local government organizations, of varying size and rural/urban locations in Kansas and North Carolina, participated in the research. Response rates ranged from 43 to 86 percent (see Table A.1).

With details varying across the nine organizational participants, the typical project began with an interview process. A small number of randomly selected employees were invited to meet with researchers one-on-one at convenient off-site locations. An interview protocol guided the semi-structured conversations between researchers and employees; topics ranged from those of interest to researchers (e.g., rules) to those of interest to local government managers (diversity, performance evaluation processes, receptivity to policy changes). Interview results were transcribed and analyzed using qualitative software. All in all, 228 interviews were conducted as part of the study.

Interviews were held in the conference rooms of buildings selected for their location away from employee worksites. At the outset of each interview the researcher would explain the purposes of the study, the confidentiality of the results, and the interview consent form; the employee was given the chance to ask questions about the study. Once the researcher and employee had signed the interview consent form, the employee was asked about his or her role in the organization and the type of rules encountered in the workplace. Employees were then asked to discuss workplace rules they considered good and bad, however they defined those terms. This approach sought to give voice to the employees' perceptions of rule quality, as opposed to anchoring their responses in preexisting theory (Glaser and Strauss 1999).

Box A.1 Local Government Workplace Study Recruitment Announcement

---

Attention City/County Managers:
Study Participation Opportunity!
Good Rules, Bad Rules and Public Employees

Rules are a fact of life for public employees. Yet surprisingly little is known about how public employees perceive rules or how rules affect public employees. This information is important for understanding rule implementation and effectiveness.

During summer 2005, Assistant Professor Leisha DeHart-Davis of University of Kansas's Department of Public Administration will be conducting research on rules in public organizations. As part of the project, she seeks organizations to participate in the study.

Study participation involves interviews and mail surveys of employees. Participating organizations will provide input into research design (e.g., questions asked, rules emphasized, departments selected for study).

The benefits to your organization include:

✓ Feedback on rules, both positive and negative
✓ Information on employee perspectives on rules, including their level of rule understanding and perceptions of rule legitimacy and effectiveness
✓ A memo that summarizes the research results
✓ In-person presentation of results, available upon request.

If you are interested in having your organization included in this study, please email her at lddavis@ku.edu.

The research team used patterns of interview results (where three or more employees made similar comments) to develop survey instruments. For example, one interview process identified concerns about information bottlenecks, which triggered the development of survey items about top-down communications (timeliness, adequacy, accuracy, etc.). Local government managers also provided input into the survey design, identifying topics of interest, flagging unfamiliar language, and evaluating readability.

Survey processes began with an alert letter being sent by the top administrator, which expressed support for the study and encouraged participation. Within two weeks of the initial alert, survey invitations were distributed to all

Table A.1 Local Government Workplace Study—Organizational Participants

Organization	Type of Public Organization	State	# Employees	# Survey Respondents	Survey Response Rate	Rural vs. Urban	Interviews	Survey Method	Year
1	City	Kansas	59	36	61%	Rural	20	paper	2005
2	City	Kansas	109	90	83%	Rural	20	paper	2005
3	City	Kansas	314	136	43%	Rural	20	paper	2005
4	City	Kansas	843	384	46%	Urban	30	paper	2006
5	Health Department	Kansas	127	109	86%	Urban	0	electronic	2010
6	City	Kansas	1,199	577	48%	Urban	48	paper/electronic	2010
7	City/County Government	Kansas	2,101	1,081	51%	Urban	68	paper/electronic	2010
8	Mental Health Local Management Entity	North Carolina	252	214	85%	Urban	0	electronic	2013
9	City	North Carolina	775	462	60%	Urban	22	paper/electronic	2012

employees, along with guarantees of respondent confidentiality. Communications between researchers and respondents was structured based on the Tailored Design Method for mixed mode surveys (Dillman 2000), which requires multiple contacts and consistent messages that convey the research's importance and then conveys appreciation for the research participant's time. Surveys of the participants from the first four organizations were conducted by mail; a combination of paper and electronic survey formats were used for participants from three organizations; and surveys of employees of two organizations were conducted exclusively in electronic format.

REFERENCES

Abdullah v. County of St. Louis. US District Court, Missouri, Eastern Division, 4:14-CV-01436, 2014.

Acker, Joan. 1990. "Hierarchies, Jobs, Bodies: A Theory of Gendered Organizations." *Gender and Society* 4 (2): 139–58.

Adams, G. B., and D. L. Balfour. 2009. *Unmasking Administrative Evil*. Armonk, NY: M.E. Sharpe.

Adler, Paul S. 1993. "The 'Learning Bureaucracy': New United Motor Manufacturing, Inc." In *Research in Organizational Behavior* vol. 15, edited by L. L. Cummings and Barry M. Staw, 111–94. Greenwich, CT: JAI.

———. "Building Better Bureaucracies." 1999. *Academy of Management Perspectives* 13 (4): 36–47. http://amp.aom.org/cgi/doi/10.5465/AME.1999.2570553.

———. 2012. "The Sociological Ambivalence of Bureaucracy: From Weber Via Gouldner to Marx." *Organization Science* 23 (1): 244–66. http://pubsonline.informs.org/doi/abs/10.1287/orsc.1100.0615.

Adler, Paul S., and Bryan Borys. 1996. "Two Types of Bureaucracy: Enabling and Coercive." *Administrative Science Quarterly* 41 (1): 61–89.

Aiken, Michael, and Jerald Hage. 1966. "Organizational Alienation: A Comparative Analysis." *American Sociological Review* 31 (4): 497–507.

Anderson, Cynthia D., and Donald Tomaskovic-Devey. 1995. "Patriarchal Pressures: An Exploration of Organizational Processes that Exacerbate and Erode Gender Earnings Inequality." *Work and Occupations* 22 (3): 328–56.

Ashforth, Blake E., and Yitzhak Fried. 1988. "The Mindlessness of Organizational Behaviors." *Human Relations* 41 (4): 305–29.

Bacharach, Michael, Gerardo Guerra, and Daniel Zizzo. 2001. "Is Trust Self-Fulfilling?: An Experimental Study." University of Oxford Department of Economics Discussion Paper Series no. 76.

Baehler, Karen, Aviva Chengcheng Liu, and David H. Rosenbloom. 2014. "Mission-Extrinsic Public Values as an Extension of Regime Values: Examples from the United States and the People's Republic of China." *Administration and Society*: doi: 0095399713515873.

Baker, Sally H., Amitai Etzioni, Richard A. Hansen, and Marvin Sontag. 1973. "Tolerance for Bureaucratic Structure: Theory and Measurement." *Human Relations* 26 (6): 775–86.

Barakat, Halim. 1969. "Alienation: A Process of Encounter between Utopia and Reality." *British Journal of Sociology* 20 (1): 1–10.

Barnard, Chester. 1938. *The Functions of the Executive.* Boston: Harvard University Press.

Barnett, Michael. 2002. *Eyewitness to a Genocide: The United Nations and Rwanda.* Ithaca, NY: Cornell University Press, 2002.

Baron, James N., Michael T. Hannan, Greta Hsu, and Ozgecan Kocak. 2007. "In the Company of Women: Gender Inequality and the Logic of Bureaucracy in Start-Up Firms." *Work and Occupations* 34 (1): 35–66.

Battmann, Wolfgang, and Petra Klumb. 1993. "Behavioural Economics and Compliance with Safety Regulations." *Safety Science* 16 (1): 35–46.

Beck, Nikolaus, and Alfred Kieser. 2003. "The Complexity of Rule Systems, Experience, and Organizational Learning." *Organization Studies* 24 (5): 793–814.

Becker, Markus C. 2004. "Organizational Routines: A Review of the Literature." *Industrial and Corporate Change* 13 (4): 643–78.

Bendix, Reinhard. 1977. *Nation-Building and Citizenship: Studies of Our Changing Social Order.* Berkeley, CA: University of California Press.

Bensman, J., and B. Rosenberg. 1963. *Mass, Class, and Bureaucracy: The Evolution of Contemporary Society.* Englewood Cliffs, NJ: Literary Licensing LLC.

Bielby, William T. 2000. "Minimizing Workplace Gender and Racial Bias." *Contemporary Sociology* 29 (1): 120–29.

Bies, Robert J., and Tom R. Tyler. 1993. "The 'Litigation Mentality' in Organizations: A Test of Alternative Psychological Explanations." *Organization Science* 4 (3): 352–66.

Bigley, Gregory A., Lyman W. Porter, and Richard M. Steers. 2003. *Motivation and Work Behavior.* Boston: McGraw-Hill/Irwin.

Bijlsma-Frankema, Katinka, and Rosalinde Klein Woolthuis. 2005. *Trust Under Pressure: Empirical Investigations of Trust and Trust Building in Uncertain Circumstances.* Northampton, MA: Edward Elgar.

Blau, Peter. 1963. *The Dynamics of Bureaucracy: A Study of Interpersonal Relations in Two Government Agencies.* Rev. ed. Chicago: University of Chicago Press.

———. 1974. *On the Nature of Organizations.* New York: Wiley.

Blau, Peter Michael, and W. Richard Scott. 1962. *Formal Organizations: A Comparative Approach.* Stanford, CA: Stanford University Press.

Borry, Erin. 2013. "Rule Bending and Red Tape: Organizational and Individual Influences and the Effect of Ethical Climate." PhD dissertation, University of Kansas.

———. 2016. "A New Measure of Red Tape: Introducing the Three Item Red Tape (TIRT) Scale." *International Public Management Journal* 19 (4): 573–93.

Borry, Erin, and Leisha DeHart-Davis. 2015. "A Legitimacy Model of Organizational Rules." Paper presented at the University of Minnesota Public Management Research Conference, Minneapolis, June 11–13.

Borry, Erin, Leisha DeHart-Davis, Wesley Kaufmann, Cullen Merritt, Zachary T. Mohr, and Lars G. Tummers. 2016. "Organizational Rule Attributes and Compliance: A Multi-Method Green Tape Study." December 1. Available at SSRN: https://ssrn.com/abstract=2879136.

Bourrier, M. 1999. "Constructing Organisational Reliability: The Problem of Embeddedness and Duality." In *Nuclear Safety: A Human Factors Perspective*, edited by J. Misumi, B. Wilpert, and R. Miller, 25–48. London: Taylor & Francis.

Boyne, George A. 2002. "Public and Private Management: What's the Difference?" *Journal of Management Studies* 39 (1): 97–122.

Bozeman, Barry. 1987. *All Organizations Are Public: Bridging Public and Private Organizational Theories*. The Jossey-Bass Management Series. San Francisco: Jossey Bass.

———. 1993. "A Theory of Government 'Red Tape.'" *Journal of Public Administration and Theory* 3 (3): 273–304.

———. 2000. *Bureaucracy and Red Tape*. Upper Saddle River, NJ: Prentice Hall.

———. 2007. *Public Values and Public Interest: Counterbalancing Economic Individualism*. Washington, DC: Georgetown University Press.

Bozeman, Barry, and Derrick M. Anderson. 2014. "Public Policy and the Origins of Bureaucratic Red Tape: Implications of the Stanford Yacht Scandal." *Administration and Society* 46 (1): 1–24.

Bozeman, Barry, and Leisha DeHart-Davis. 1999. "Red Tape and Clean Air: Title V Air Pollution Permitting Implementation as a Test Bed for Theory Development." *Journal of Public Administration Research and Theory* 9 (1): 141–78.

Bozeman, Barry, and Mary Feeney. 2011. *Rules and Red Tape: A Prism for Public Administration Theory and Research*. Armonk, NY: M.E. Sharpe.

Bozeman, Barry, and Gordon Kingsley. 1998. "Risk Culture in Public and Private Organizations." *Public Administration Review* 58 (2): 109–18.

Bozeman, Barry, and Hal G. Rainey. 1998. "Organizational Rules and the 'Bureaucratic Personality.'" *American Journal of Political Science* 42 (1): 163–89.

Bozeman, Barry, Pamela N. Reed, and Patrick Scott. 1992. "Red Tape and Task Delays in Public and Private Organizations." *Administration and Society* 24 (3): 290–322.

Braithwaite, John, and Toni Makkai. 1994. "Trust and Compliance." *Policing and Society* 4 (1): 1–12.

Brehm, John O., and Scott Gates. 1997. *Working, Shirking, and Sabotage: Bureaucratic Response to a Democratic Public*. Ann Arbor: University of Michigan Press.

Brewer, Gene A., and Richard M. Walker. 2009. "The Impact of Red Tape on Governmental Performance: An Empirical Analysis." *Journal of Public Administration Research and Theory* 20 (1): 233–57.

Brill, Steven. 2003. *After: How America Confronted the September 12 Era*. New York: Simon and Schuster.

Brockmann, Julia. 2015. "Unbureaucratic Behavior among Street-Level Bureaucrats: The Case of the German State Police." *Review of Public Personnel Administration*, 1–22.

Brockner, Joel, and P. A. Siegel. 1996. "Understanding the Interaction between

Procedural and Distributive Justice: The Role of Trust." In *Trust in Organizations: Frontiers of Theory and Research*, edited by Roderick M. Kramer and Tom R. Tyler, 390–413. Thousand Oaks, CA: SAGE.

Brodkin, E. Z., and M. Majmundar. 2010. "Administrative Exclusion: Organizations and the Hidden Costs of Welfare Claiming." *Journal of Public Administration Research and Theory* 20 (4): 827–48.

Brown, Don W. 1974. "Cognitive Development and Willingness to Comply with Law." *American Journal of Political Science* 18 (3): 583–94.

Bryant, Phil C., Charlotte A. Davis, Julie I. Hancock, and James M. Vardaman. 2010. "When Rule Makers Become Rule Breakers: Employee Level Outcomes of Managerial Pro-Social Rule Breaking." *Employee Responsibilities and Rights Journal* 22 (2): 101–12.

Buchanan, Bruce, II. 1975. "Red Tape and the Service Ethic." *Administration and Society* 6 (4): 423–44.

Carpenter, Ted Galen, and Charles V. Pena. 2008. "A Useless and Intrusive PR Display." In *Smart Power: Toward a Prudent Foreign Policy for America*, 246–47. Washington, DC: Cato Institute.

Chemerinsky, Erwin, Jolene Forman, Allen Hopper, and Sam Kamin. 2015. "Cooperative Federalism and Marijuana Regulation." *UCLA Law Review* 62 (1) (January 1): 74.

Chen, Chung-An, and Hal G. Rainey. 2013. "Personnel Formalization and the Enhancement of Teamwork: A Public–Private Comparison." *Public Management Review* 16 (7): 945–68.

Child, John. 1972. "Organization Structure and Strategies of Control: A Replication of the Aston Study." *Administrative Science Quarterly* 17 (2): 163–77.

Clegg, Stewart. 1981. "Organization and Control." *Administrative Science Quarterly*: 545–62.

Clegg, Stewart, and David Dunkerly. 1987. *Organization, Class, and Control*. London: Routledge & Kegan Paul.

Cohen, Harry. 1965. *The Demonics of Bureaucracy: Problems of Change in a Government Agency*. Ames: Iowa State University Press.

———. 1970. "Bureaucratic Flexibility: Some Comments on Robert Merton's 'Bureaucratic Structure and Personality.'" *British Journal of Sociology* 21 (4): 390–99.

Cohen, Michael D., and Paul Bacdayan. 1994. "Organizational Routines Are Stored as Procedural Memory: Evidence from a Laboratory Study." *Organization Science* 5 (4): 554–68.

Cohen, Michael D., Roger Burkhart, Giovanni Dosi, Massimo Egidi, Luigi Marengo, Massimo Warglien, and Sidney Winter. 1996. "Routines and Other Recurring Action Patterns of Organizations: Contemporary Research Issues." *Industrial and Corporate Change* 5 (3): 653–98.

Cohen, Michael D., James G. March, and Johan P. Olsen. 1972. "A Garbage Can Model of Organizational Choice." *Administrative Science Quarterly* 17 (1): 1–25.

Cohen, S., and R. Brand. 1993. *Total Quality Management in Government: A Practical Guide for the Real World*. San Francisco: Jossey-Bass.

Cohen, S. and W. B. Eimicke. 1998. *Tools for Innovators: Creative Strategies for Managing Public Sector Organizations.* San Francisco: Jossey-Bass.

Colvin, Alexander J. S. 2003. "The Dual Transformation of Workplace Dispute Resolution." *Industrial Relations* 42 (4): 712–35.

Cook, Clarissa, and Malcolm Waters. 1998. "The Impact of Organizational Form on Gendered Labour Markets in Engineering and Law." *Sociological Review* 46 (2): 314–39.

Crosby, Benjamin L. 1996. "Policy Implementation: The Organizational Challenge." *World Development* 24 (9): 1403–15.

Crozier, Michel. 1964. *The Bureaucratic Phenomenon.* Chicago: University of Chicago Press.

———. 2009. *The Bureaucratic Phenomenon.* Brunswick, NJ: Transaction.

Cyert, R. M., and J. G. March. 1963. *A Behavioural View of the Firm.* Englewood Cliffs, NJ: Prentice-Hall.

Dahling, Jason J., Samantha L. Chau, David M. Mayer, and Jane B. Gregory. 2012. "Breaking Rules for the Right Reasons? An Investigation of Pro-Social Rule Breaking." *Journal of Organizational Behavior* 33 (1): 21–42.

Dalton, Melville. 1987. *Men Who Manage: Fusions of Feeling and Theory in Administration.* Reprint, New York: Garland.

———. 2013. *Men Who Manage: Fusions of Feeling and Theory in Administration.* New Brunswick, NJ: Transaction.

Davis, Randall S. 2012. "Union Commitment and Stakeholder Red Tape: How Union Values Shape Perceptions of Organizational Rules." *Review of Public Personnel Administration:* doi 10.11770734371X12453056.

Deal, Terrence E., and Allan A. Kennedy. 1982. *Corporate Cultures: The Rites and Rituals of Organizational Life.* Reading, PA: Addison-Wesley.

De Cremer, David, and Tom R. Tyler. 2005. "Managing Group Behavior: The Interplay between Procedural Justice, Sense of Self, and Cooperation." *Advances in Experimental Social Psychology* 37: 151–218.

Deephouse, David L., and Mark Suchman. 2008. "Legitimacy in Organizational Institutionalism." In *The SAGE Handbook of Organizational Institutionalism,* edited by Royston Greenwood, Christine Oliver, Kerstin Sahlin, and Roy Suddaby, 49–77. Thousand Oaks, CA: SAGE.

DeHart-Davis, Leisha. 2007. "The Unbureaucratic Personality." *Public Administration Review* 67 (5): 892–903.

———. 2009a. "Green Tape: A Theory of Effective Organizational Rules." *Journal of Public Administration Research and Theory* 19 (2): 361–84.

———. 2009b. "Can Bureaucracy Benefit Organizational Women? An Exploratory Study." *Administration and Society* 41 (3): 340–63.

———. 2009c. "Green Tape and Public Employee Rule Abidance: Why Organizational Rule Attributes Matter." *Public Administration Review* 69 (5): 901–10.

DeHart-Davis, L., E. Borry, W. Kaufmann, L. Tummers, Z. Mohr, and C. Merritt. 2015. "Organizational Rule Attributes and Compliance: A Multi-Method Green Tape Study," December 1. Available at SSRN: https://ssrn.com/abstract.

DeHart-Davis, Leisha, and Barry Bozeman. 2001. "Regulatory Compliance and Air Quality Permitting: Why Do Firms Overcomply?" *Journal of Public Administration Research and Theory* 11 (4): 471–508.

DeHart-Davis, Leisha, Jie Chen, and Todd D. Little. 2013. "Written Versus Unwritten Rules: The Role of Rule Formalization in Green Tape." *International Public Management Journal* 16 (3): 331–56.

DeHart-Davis, Leisha, Randall S. Davis, and Zachary Mohr. 2014. "Green Tape and Job Satisfaction: Can Organizational Rules Make Employees Happy?" *Journal of Public Administration Research and Theory* 25 (3): 849–76.

DeHart-Davis, Leisha, Drake Maynard, and Meagan McDougall. 2015. "From Red Tape to Green Tape: Improving due Process in Local Government Organizations." Local Government Research Collaborative, University of North Carolina School of Government, Chapel Hill, North Carolina.

DeHart-Davis, Leisha, and Sanjay K. Pandey. 2005. "Red Tape and Public Employees: Does Perceived Rule Dysfunction Alienate Managers?" *Journal of Public Administration Research and Theory* 15 (1): 133–48.

Denhardt, Robert, Janet Denhardt, and Maria Aristigueta. 2012. *Managing Human Behavior in Public and Nonprofit Organizations.* Los Angeles: SAGE.

Denison, Daniel R. 1996. "What Is the Difference between Organizational Culture and Organizational Climate? A Native's Point of View on a Decade of Paradigm Wars." *Academy of Management Review* 21 (3): 619–54.

Dillman, Don A. 2000. *Mail and Internet Surveys: The Tailored Design Method.* Vol. 2. New York: Wiley.

DiMaggio, Paul J., and Walter W. Powell. 1983. "The Iron Cage Revisited: Institutional Isomorphism and Collective Rationality in Organizational Fields." *American Sociological Association* 48 (2): 147–60.

Diver, Colin. 1982. "Engineers and Entrepreneurs: The Dilemma of Public Management." *Journal of Policy Analysis and Management* 1 (3): 402–6.

Dobbin, Frank, Lauren B. Edelman, John William Meyer, and Ann Swidler. 1988. "The Expansion of Due Process in Organizations." In *Institutional Patterns and Organizations: Culture and Environment,* edited by Lynne G. Zucker, 71–98. Cambridge, MA: Ballinger.

Donaldson, Lex. 2001. *The Contingency Theory of Organizations.* Thousand Oaks, CA: SAGE.

Dow, Thomas E. 1969. "The Theory of Charisma." *Sociological Quarterly* 10 (3): 306–18.

Downs, Anthony. 1967. *Inside Bureaucracy.* Santa Monica, CA: RAND Corporation.

Drost, D. A., and F. P. O'Brien. 1983. "Are There Grievances Against Your Non-Union Grievance Procedure? A Discussion of Avoidable Mistakes." *Personnel Administrator* 28 (1): 36–42.

Duerst-Lahti, Georgia, and Rita Mae Kelly. 1995. *Gender Power, Leadership, and Governance.* Ann Arbor: University of Michigan Press.

Edelman, Lauren B. 1990. "Legal Environments and Organizational Governance: The Expansion of Due Process in the American Workplace." *American Journal of Sociology* 95 (6): 1401–40.

———. 1992. "Legal Ambiguity and Symbolic Structures: Organizational Mediation of Civil Rights Law." *American Journal of Sociology* 97 (6): 1531–76.

Edelman, Lauren B., and Stephen M. Petterson. 1999. "Symbols and Substance in Organizational Response to Civil Rights Law." *Research in Social Stratification and Mobility* 17: 107–38.

Edelman, Lauren B., Christopher Uggen, and Howard S. Erlanger. 1999. "The Endogeneity of Legal Regulation: Grievance Procedures as Rational Myth." *American Journal of Sociology* 105 (2): 406–54.

Ellickson, Robert. 2009. *Order without Law: How Neighbors Settle Disputes.* Cambridge, MA: Harvard University Press.

Elvira, Marta M., and Mary E. Graham. 2002. "Not Just a Formality: Pay System Formalization and Sex-Related Earnings Effects." *Organization Science* 13 (6): 601–17.

Engel, Gloria V. 1969. "The Effect of Bureaucracy on the Professional Autonomy of the Physician." *Journal of Health and Social Behavior* 10 (1): 30–41.

Erikson, Kai. 1986. "On Work and Alienation." *American Sociological Review* 51 (1): 1–8.

Evans, Tony. 2012a. "Organisational Rules and Discretion in Adult Social Work." *British Journal of Social Work* 43 (4): 739–58.

———. 2012b. *Professional Discretion in Welfare Services: Beyond Street-Level Bureaucracy.* Burlington, VT: Ashgate.

Evans, Tony, and John Harris. 2004. "Street-Level Bureaucracy, Social Work, and the (Exaggerated) Death of Discretion." *British Journal of Social Work* 34 (6): 871–95.

Evans, Tony, and Mark Hardy. 2010. *Evidence and Knowledge for Practice*, vol. 1. Cambridge, UK: Polity.

Ewing, David. 1989. *Justice on the Job: Resolving Grievances in the Nonunion Workplace.* Boston: Harvard Business School Press.

Falk, Armin, and Michael Kosfeld. 2004. "The Hidden Cost of Control." IZA Discussion Paper no. 1203 (IEW working paper no. 193), 24.

Feldman, Martha S. 2000. "Organizational Routines as a Source of Continuous Change." *Organization Science* 11 (6): 611–29.

Feldman, Martha S., and Brian T. Pentland. 2003. "Reconceptualizing Organizational Routines as a Source of Flexibility and Change." *Administrative Science Quarterly* 48 (1): 94–118.

Ferguson, Ann. 1984. "Sex War: The Debate between Radical and Libertarian Feminists." *Signs* 10 (1): 106–12.

Feuille, Peter, and Denise R. Chachere. 1995. "Looking Fair or Being Fair: Remedial Voice Procedures in Nonunion Workplaces." *Journal of Management* 21 (1): 27–42.

Flower, Linda, and John R. Hayes. 1981. "A Cognitive Process Theory of Writing." *College Composition and Communication* 32 (4): 365–87.

Folger, Robert. 1977. "Distributive and Procedural Justice: Combined Impact of Voice and Improvement on Experienced Inequity." *Journal of Personality and Social Psychology* 35 (2): 108-119. doi:10.1037/0022-3514.35.2.108.

Follett, Mary Parker. 1987 [1949]. *Freedom and Co-Ordination: Lectures in Business Organization.* New York: Management Publications Trust.

———. 2015. *Creative Experience.* New York: Longmans, Green.

Fountain, Jane E. 2001. "Paradoxes of Public Sector Customer Service." *Governance* 14 (1): 55–73.

Franklin, Aimee L., and Javier F. Pagan. 2006. "Organization Culture as an Explanation for Employee Discipline Practices." *Review of Public Personnel Administration* 26 (1): 52–73.

Frederickson, H. George. 2010. *Social Equity and Public Administration Origins, Developments, and Applications.* Armonk, NY: M.E. Sharpe.

Frederickson, H. George, Kevin Smith, Christopher W. Larimer, and Michael Licari. 2015. *The Public Administration Theory Primer.* Boulder, CO: Westview.

Freeman, Jo. 1972. "The Tyranny of Structurelessness." *Berkeley Journal of Sociology* 17: 151–64.

Freidin, Jesse, and Francis J. Ulman. 1945. "Arbitration and the National War Labor Board." *Harvard Law Review* 58 (3): 309–60.

French, John R. P., Jr., and Bertram Raven. 1959. "The Bases of Social Power." In *Studies in Social Power,* edited by Dorwin P. Cartwright, 150–67. Ann Arbor: University of Michigan Institute for Social Research.

Frey, Bruno S. 1993. "Shirking or Work Morale?: The Impact of Regulating." *European Economic Review* 37 (8): 1523–32.

Gagliano, Mike, Casey Phillips, and Phillip Jose. 2008. *Air Management for the Fire Service.* Tulsa, OK: Pennwell.

Galbraith, Jay. 1977. *Organization Design.* Reading, PA: Addison-Wesley.

Geuras, Dean, and Charles Garofalo. 2005. *Practical Ethics in Public Administration.* Vienna, VA: Management Concepts.

Gilligan, Carol. 1982. *In a Different Voice: Psychological Theory and Women's Development.* Cambridge, MA: Harvard University Press.

Glaser, Barney G., and Anselm L. Strauss. 1999. *The Discovery of Grounded Theory: Strategies for Qualitative Research.* Piscataway, NJ: AldineTransaction.

Goldmann, Kjell. 2005. "Appropriateness and Consequences: The Logic of Neo-Institutionalism." *Governance* 18 (1): 35–52.

Goodsell, Charles. 2003. *The Case for Bureaucracy: A Public Administration Polemic.* Washington, DC: SAGE.

———. 2000. "Red Tape and a Theory of Bureaucratic Rules." *Public Administration Review* 60 (4): 373–75.

———. 2014. *The New Case for Bureaucracy.* Washington, DC: SAGE.

Goody, Jack. 1986. *The Logic of Writing and the Organization of Society.* Cambridge, UK: Cambridge University Press.

Goody, Jack, and Ian Watt. 1963. "The Consequences of Literacy." *Comparative Studies in Society and History* 5 (3): 304–45.

Goody, Jack. 1975. Literacy in Traditional Societies. Cambridge, Eng.; UK: Cambridge University Press.

Gouldner, Alvin. 1952. "On Weber's Analysis of Bureaucratic Rules." In *Reader in Bureaucracy*, edited by Robert K. Merton, 48–52. Glencoe, IL: Free Press.

———. 1954. *Patterns of Industrial Bureaucracy*. New York: Free Press.

———. 1964. *Patterns of Industrial Bureaucracy*. New York: Free Press.

Graham, Pauline. 2003. *Mary Parker Follett—Prophet of Management: A Celebration of Writings from the 1920s*. Reprint, Washington, DC: Beard.

Greenberg, Jerald, and Robert Folger. 1983. "Procedural Justice, Participation, and the Fair Process Effect in Groups and Organizations." In *Basic Group Processes*, edited by Paul. B. Paulus, 235–56. New York: Springer.

Gregg, Richard B. 1919. "The National War Labor Board." *Harvard Law Review* 33 (1): 39–63.

Griffin, Ricky, and Gregory Moorhead. 2011. *Organizational Behavior*. Mason, OH: Cengage Learning.

Grimaldi, Rosa, and Salvatore Torrisi. 2001. "Codified-Tacit and General-Specific Knowledge in the Division of Labour among Firms: A Study of the Software Industry." *Research Policy* 30 (9): 1425–42. http://www.sciencedirect.com/science/article/pii/S0048733301001603.

Guerra, Gerardo A., and Daniel John Rizzo. 2004. "Trust Responsiveness and Beliefs." *Journal of Economic Behavior and Organization* 55: 25–30.

Guy, Mary Ellen, and Meredith A. Newman. 2004. "Women's Jobs, Men's Jobs: Sex Segregation and Emotional Labor." *Public Administration Review* 64 (3): 289–98.

Guy, Mary E., Meredith A. Newman, and Sharon H. Mastracci. 2008. *Emotional Labor: Putting the Service in Public Service*. Armonk, NY: Sharpe.

Guy, Mary E., Meredith A. Newman, Sharon H. Mastracci, and Steven Maynard-Moody. 2010. "Emotional Labor in the Human Service Organization." In *Human Services as Complex Organizations*, edited by Hasenfeld Yeheskel, 291–310. Thousand Oaks, CA: SAGE.

Hall, Richard H. 1963. "The Concept of Bureaucracy: An Empirical Assessment." *American Journal of Sociology* 69 (1): 32–40.

———. 1999. *Organizations: Structures, Processes, and Outcomes*. 7th ed. Upper Saddle River, NJ: Pearson.

Hannan, Michael T., and John Freeman. 1984. "Structural Inertia and Organizational Change." *American Sociological Review* 49 (2): 149–64. http://www.jstor.org/stable/2095567?seq=1#page_scan_tab_contents.

Haraway, William M., III. 2002. "Rediscovering Process Values in Employee Grievance Procedures." *Administration and Society* 34 (5): 499–521.

———. 2005. "Employee Grievance Programs: Understanding the Nexus between Workplace Justice, Organizational Legitimacy, and Successful Organizations." *Public Personnel Management* 34 (4): 329–42.

Harris, Milton, and Artur Raviv. 2002. "Organization Design." *Management Science* 48 (7): 852–65.

Hasselbladh, Hans, and Jannis Kallinikos. 2000. "The Project of Rationalization: A Critique and Reappraisal of Neo-Institutionalism in Organization Studies." *Organization Studies* 21 (4): 697–720.

Havelock, Eric. 1986. *The Muse Learns to Write: Reflections on Orality and Literacy from Antiquity to the Present.* New Haven, CT: Yale University Press.

Hayward, Tansy. 2010. "Practitioner's Perspective—Managing for 2020: An Exploration of Role Interdependence and Balance." *Public Administration Review* 70 (1): 136.

Head, Brian, and John Alford. 2008. "Wicked Problems: The Implications for Public Management." Australian Political Studies Association Conference Proceedings.

Heidelberg, R. 2015. "The Power of Knowing the Rules." *American Review of Public Administration,* doi:10.1177/0275074015575353.

Henderson, Alexander C. 2013. "Examining Policy Implementation in Health Care: Rule Abidance and Deviation in Emergency Medical Services." *Public Administration Review* 73 (6): 799–809.

Hrebiniak, Lawrence G. 1974. "Job Technology, Supervision, and Work-Group Structure." *Administrative Science Quarterly* (1974): 395–410.

Hummel, Ralph P. 1994. *The Bureaucratic Experience: A Critique of Life in the Modern Organization.* 4th ed. New York: St. Martin's.

———. 2008. *The Bureaucratic Experience: The Post-Modern Challenge.* 5th ed. Armonk, NY: M.E. Sharpe.

Hutchinson, Sally A. 1990. "Responsible Subversion: A Study of Rule-Bending among Nurses." *Research and Theory for Nursing Practice* 4 (1): 3–17.

Jablin, Fredric. 1987. "Formal Organization Structure." In *Handbook of Organizational Communication: An Interdisciplinary Perspective,* edited by F. M. Jablin, L. L. Putnam, Karlene Roberts, and Lyman Porter, 389–419. Newbury Park, CA: SAGE.

Jackson, John H., and Susan W. Adams. 1979. "The Life Cycle of Rules." *Academy of Management Review* 4 (2): 269–73.

Jackson, Susan E., and Randall S. Schuler. 1985. "A Meta-Analysis and Conceptual Critique of Research on Role Ambiguity and Role Conflict in Work Settings." *Organizational Behavior and Human Decision Processes* 36 (1): 16–78.

Jakobsen, Mads L. F., and Peter B. Mortensen. 2015. "Rules and the Doctrine of Performance Management." *Public Administration Review* 76 (2): 302–12.

Jensen, M., and W. Mecklin. 1976. "Theory of the Firm: Manager Behaviour, Agency Costs, and Analogous Situations." *Journal of Financial Economics* 3: 323–29.

Jewson, Nick, and David Mason. 1986. "Modes of Discrimination in the Recruitment Process: Formalisation, Fairness, and Efficiency." *Sociology* 20 (1): 43–63.

Jørgensen, Torben Beck, and Barry Bozeman. 2007. "Public Values: An Inventory." *Administration and Society* 39 (3): 354–81.

Kallinikos, J. 1996. "Predictable Worlds: On Writing, Accountability, and Other Things." *Scandinavian Journal of Management* 12 (1): 7–24.

Kant, Immanuel, and Paul Guyer. 1998. *Critique of Pure Reason.* Cambrdige, UK: Cambridge University Press.

Kanter, Rosabeth Moss. 1977. *Men and Women of the Corporation.* New York: Basic.

Kanungo, Rabindra N. 1979. "The Concepts of Alienation and Involvement Revisited." *Psychological Bulletin* 86 (1): 119–38.

Katz, Daniel, and Robert Louis Kahn. 1978. *The Social Psychology of Organizations.* 2nd ed. New York: John Wiley and Sons. http://catalog.hathitrust.org.libproxy.lib.unc .edu/api/volumes/oclc/3558969.html.

Kaufman, Herbert. 1960. *The Forest Ranger: A Study in Administrative Behavior.* Washington, DC: Resources for the Future.

———. 1977. *Red Tape: Its Origins, Uses, and Abuses.* Washington, DC: Brookings Institution.

———. 2006. *The Forest Ranger: A Study in Administrative Behavior.* Washington, DC: Resources for the Future.

Khademian, Anne. 1997. *Working with Culture: The Way the Job Gets Done in Public Programs.* Washington, DC: CQ.

———. 2001. "Is Silly Putty Manageable? Looking for the Links between Culture, Management, and Context." In *Advancing Public Management: New Developments in Theory, Methods, and Practice,* edited by Jeffrey Brudney, Laurence O'Toole Jr., and Hal Rainey, 33–48: Washington, DC: Georgetown University Press.

Kieser, Alfred, Nikolaus Beck, and Risto Tainio. 2001. "Rules and Organizational Learning: The Behavioral Theory Approach." In *Handbook of Organizational Learning and Knowledge,* 598–623. Oxford, UK: Oxford University Press.

Kieser, Alfred, and Ulrich Koch. 2008. "Bounded Rationality and Organizational Learning Based on Rule Changes." *Management Learning* 39 (3): 329–47.

Kirby, Erika, and Kathleen Krone. 2002. "'The Policy Exists but You Can't Really Use It': Communication and the Structuration of Work-Family Policies." *Journal of Applied Communication Research* 30 (1): 50–77.

Klaas, B. S., and A. S. DeNisi. 1989. "Managerial Reactions to Employee Dissent: The Impact of Grievance Activity on Performance Rating." *Academy of Management Journal* 32 (4): 705–17.

Kostova, Tatiana, and Kendall Roth. 2002. "Adoption of an Organizational Practice by Subsidiaries of Multinational Corporations: Institutional and Relational Effects." *Academy of Management Journal* 45 (1): 215–33.

Kristof, Amy L. 1996. "Person-Organization Fit: An Integrative Review of Its Conceptualizations, Measurement, and Implications." *Personnel Psychology* 49 (1): 1–49.

Lan, Zhiyong, and Hal G. Rainey. 1992. "Goals, Rules, and Effectiveness in Public, Private, and Hybrid Organizations: More Evidence on Frequent Assertions about Differences." *Journal of Public Administration Research and Theory* 2 (1): 5–28.

Landau, Martin, and Russell Stout Jr. 1979. "To Manage Is Not to Control: Or the Folly of Type II Errors." *Public Administration Review* 39 (2): 148–56.

Latos, Allison. "9 Investigates: City Employees Call Grievance Process Unfair." At wsoctv.com., http://www.wsoctv.com/news/news/special-reports/9-investigates -city-employees-call-grievance-proce/njFpQ/.

Lawton, Rebecca. 1998. "Not Working to Rule: Understanding Procedural Violations at Work." *Safety Science* 28 (2): 77–95.

Leek, Joanne D., David M. Saunders, and Sylvie de St. Onge. 1992. "Achieving a Diversified Workforce with Employment Equity Programs: Effects on Hiring Women." *Academy of Management Proceedings* 1992 (1): 385–89.

Lehman, David W., and Rangaraj Ramanujam. 2009. "Selectivity in Organizational Rule Violations." *Academy of Management Review* 34 (4): 643–57.

Leidner, Robin. 1993. *Fast Food, Fast Talk: Service Work and the Routinization of Everyday Life*. Berkeley: University of California Press, 1993.

Leivesley, Robert, Adrian Can, and Alexander Kouzmin. 1994. "Ethnocentric Mishandling, Or How Weber Became a Management Consultant." *Handbook of Bureaucracy* 55: 41.

Leventhal, Gerald S. 1980. "What Should Be Done with Equity Theory?" In *Social Exchange: Advances in Theory and Research*, edited by Kenneth J. Gergen, Martin S. Greenberg, and Richard H. Willis, 27–55. New York: Springer US.

Levitt, Barbara, and James G. March. 1988. "Organizational Learning." *Annual Review of Sociology* 14: 319–40. http://www.jstor.org/stable/2083321?seq=1#page_scan _tab_contents.

Lewin, David, and Richard B. Peterson. 1999. "Behavioral Outcomes of Grievance Activity." *Industrial Relations* 38 (4): 554–76.

Lewis-Beck, Michael S., and John R. Alford. 1980. "Can Government Regulate Safety? The Coal Mine Example." *American Political Science Review* 74 (3): 745–56. http:// www.jstor.org/stable/1958155?origin=crossref.

Li, Peter Ping, Yuntao Bai, and Youmin Xi. 2012. "The Contextual Antecedents of Organizational Trust: A Multidimensional Cross-Level Analysis." *Management and Organization Review* 8 (2): 371–96.

Linnehan, Frank, and Alison M. Konrad. 1999. "Diluting Diversity: Implications for Intergroup Inequality in Organizations." *Journal of Management Inquiry* 8 (4): 399–414.

Lipsky, Michael. 1980. *Street-Level Bureaucracy: Dilemmas of the Individual in Public Services*. New York: Russell Sage Foundation.

Long, Christopher P. 2010. "Control to Cooperation: Examining the Role of Managerial Authority in Portfolios of Managerial Actions." In *Organizational Control*, edited by Sim Sitkin, Laura Cardinal, and Katinka Bijlsma-Frankema, 365–95. Cambridge, UK: Cambridge University Press.

Lowery, Wesley. 2014. "Federal Judges Tosses 'Five Second Rule' Being Used to Police Ferguson Protests." *Washington Post*, October 6.

Lum, Cynthia, and George Fachen. 2008. *Police Pursuits in an Age of Innovation and Reform*. Alexandria, VA: International Association of Chiefs of Police.

Mael, Fred, and Blake E. Ashforth. 1992. "Alumni and Their Alma Mater: A Partial Test of the Reformulated Model of Organizational Identification." *Journal of Organizational Behavior* 13 (2): 103–23. doi:10.1002/job.4030130202.

Manning, Peter K. 1977. "Rules in Organizational Context: Narcotics Law Enforcement in Two Settings." *Sociological Quarterly* 18 (1): 44–61.

March, James. 1994. *A Primer on Decision Making: How Decisions Happen.* New York: Simon and Schuster.

———. 2008. *Explorations in Organizations.* Stanford, CA: Stanford University Press.

March, James G., and Johan P. Olsen. 1983. "The New Institutionalism: Organizational Factors in Political Life." *American Political Science Review* 78 (3): 734–49.

———. 1995. *Democratic Governance.* New York: Free Press.

———. 2004. *The Logic of Appropriateness.* Edited by Advanced Research on the Europeanisation of the Nation-State. Oslo: ARENA.

March, James G., Martin Schulz, and Xueguang Zhou. 2000. *The Dynamics of Rules: Change in Written Organizational Codes.* Stanford, CA: Stanford University Press.

March, James G., and Herbert A. Simon. 1958. *Organizations.* Oxford, UK: Wiley.

———. 1993. *Organizations.* 2nd ed. Oxford, UK: Wiley.

Mastracci, Sharon H., Mary E. Guy, and Meredith A. Newman. 2012. *Emotional Labor and Crisis Response: Working on the Razor's Edge.* Armonk, NY: M.E. Sharpe.

Maynard-Moody, Steven, and Michael Musheno. 2003. *Cops, Teachers, Counselors: Stories from the Front Lines of Public Service.* Ann Arbor: University of Michigan Press.

Maynard-Moody, Steven, and Shannon Portillo. 2010. "Street-Level Bureaucracy Theory." In *The Oxford Handbook of American Bureaucracy,* edited by Robert Durant, 252–77. Oxford, UK: Oxford University Press.

McCabe, Douglas M. 1997. "Alternative Dispute Resolution and Employee Voice in Nonunion Employment: An Ethical Analysis of Organizational Due Process Procedures and Mechanisms—The Case of the United States." *Journal of Business Ethics* 16 (3): 349–56.

McGuire, Michael. 2002. "Managing Networks: Propositions on What Managers Do and Why They Do It." *Public Administration Review* 62 (5): 599–609.

McGuire, Michael, and Chris Silvia. 2010. "The Effect of Problem Severity, Managerial and Organizational Capacity, and Agency Structure on Intergovernmental Collaboration: Evidence from Local Emergency Management." *Public Administration Review* 70 (2): 279–88.

McIlwee, J. S., and J. G. Robinson. 1992. *Women in Engineering: Gender, Power, and Workplace Culture.* Albany: State University of New York Press.

McPhee, Robert D. 1985. "Formal Structure and Organizational Communication." In *Handbook of Organizational Communication: An Interdisciplinary Perspective,* edited by F. M. Jablin, L. L. Putnam, Karlene Roberts, and Lyman Porter, 149–77. Beverly Hills, CA: SAGE.

——— 2004. "Text, Agency, and Organization in the Light of Structuration Theory." *Organization* 11 (3): 355–71.

Merton, Robert K. 1940. "Bureaucratic Structure and Personality." *Social Forces* 18 (4): 560–68.

Meyer, John W., and Brian Rowan. 1977. "Institutionalized Organizations: Formal Structure as Myth and Ceremony." *American Journal of Sociology* 83 (2): 340–63.

Meyers, Marcia K., Bonnie Glaser, and Karin MacDonald. 1998. "On the Front Lines of Welfare Delivery: Are Workers Implementing Policy Reforms?" *Journal of Policy Analysis and Management* 17 (1): 1–22.

Mills, Albert J., and Stephen J. Murgatroyd. 1991. *Organizational Rules: A Framework for Understanding Organizational Action.* Suffolk, VA: Open University Press.

Mintzberg, Henry. 1979. "The Structuring of Organizations. Englewood Cliffs, NJ: Prentice-Hall.

Mitchell, Ronald K., Bradley R. Agle, and Donna J. Wood. 1997. "Toward a Theory of Stakeholder Identification and Salience: Defining the Principle of Who and What Really Counts." *Academy of Management Review* 22 (4): 853–86.

Morrison, Elizabeth W. 2006. "Doing the Job Well: An Investigation of Pro-Social Rule Breaking." *Journal of Management* 32 (1): 5–28.

Moynihan, Donald P., and Pamela Herd. 2010. "Red Tape and Democracy: How Rules Affect Citizenship Rights." *American Review of Public Administration* 40 (6): 654–70.

Moynihan, Donald P., and Sanjay K. Pandey. 2006. "Creating Desirable Organizational Characteristics." *Public Management Review* 8 (1): 119–40.

———. 2007. "The Role of Organizations in Fostering Public Service Motivation." *Public Administration Review* 67 (1): 40–53.

Mulder, Fran. 1971. "Characteristics of Violators of Formal Company Rules." *Journal of Applied Psychology* 55 (5): 500–502.

Nelson, Richard, and Sidney Winter. 1982. *An Evolutionary Theory of Economic Change.* London: Harvard University Press.

Nesbit, Rebecca, Stephanie Moulton, Scott Robinson, Craig Smith, Leisha DeHart-Davis, Mary K. Feeney, Beth Gazley, and Yilin Hou. 2010. "Wrestling with Intellectual Diversity in Public Administration: Avoiding Disconnectedness and Fragmentation While Seeking Rigor, Depth, and Relevance." *Journal of Public Administration Research and Theory* 21 (supplement 1): i28.

Ocasio, W. 1997. "Towards an Attention-based View of the Firm." *Strategic Management Journal* 18: 187.

O'Leary, Rosemary. 1994. "The Bureaucratic Politics Paradox: The Case of Wetlands Legislation in Nevada." *Journal of Public Administration Research and Theory* 4 (4): 443–67.

———. 2014. *The Ethics of Dissent: Managing Guerrilla Government.* Thousand Oaks, CA: CQ Press.

O'Leary, Rosemary, and Heidi Koenig. 1994. "Toward a Theory of the Impact of Courts on Public Management." *Research in Public Administration* 3: 175–99.

Oberfield, Zachary. 2014. *Becoming Bureaucrats: Socialization at the Front Lines of Government Service.* Philadelphia: University of Pennsylvania Press.

Olsen, Johan. 2006. "Maybe It Is Time to Rediscover Bureaucracy." *Journal of Public Administration Research and Theory* 16 (1): 1–24.

———. 2008. "Explorations in Institutions and Logistics of Appropriateness: An Introductory Essay." In *Explorations in Organizations,* edited by James G. March. Stanford, CA: Stanford University Press.

Ong, Walter. 2013. *Orality and Literacy.* 30th anniversary ed. New York: Routledge.

Organ, Dennis, and Charles Greene. 1981. "The Effects of Formalization on Professional Involvement: A Compensatory Process Approach." *Administrative Science Quarterly* 26 (2): 237–52.

Osborne, David. 1993. "Reinventing Government." *Public Productivity and Management Review* 16 (4): 356.

Osborne, David, and Ted Gaebler. 1992. *Reinventing Government: How the Entrepreneurial Spirit Is Transforming the Public Sector.* Reading, PA: Addison-Wesley.

Osborne, David, and Peter Plastrik. 1997. *Banishing Bureaucracy: The Five Strategies for Reinventing Government.* Reading, PA: Addison-Wesley.

———. 2000. *The Reinventor's Fieldbook: Tools for Transforming Your Government.* San Francisco: Jossey-Bass.

Osiel, Mark. 2001. *Mass Atrocity, Ordinary Evil, and Hannah Arendt: Criminal Consciousness in Argentina's Dirty War.* New Haven, CT: Yale University Press.

Pandey, Sanjay K., and Gorden A. Kingsley. 2000. "Examining Red Tape in Public and Private Organizations: Alternative Explanations from a Social Psychological Model." *Journal of Public Administration Research and Theory* 10 (4): 779–800.

Pandey, Sanjay K., and Donald P. Moynihan. 2005. "Bureaucratic Red Tape and Organizational Performance: Testing the Moderating Role of Culture and Political Support." La Follette School Working Paper no. 2005-026.

Pandey, Sanjay K., and Hal G. Rainey. 2006. "Public Managers' Perceptions of Organizational Goal Ambiguity: Analyzing Alternative Models." *International Public Management Journal* 9 (2): 85–112.

Pentland, Brian T., and Henry H. Rueter. 1994. "Organizational Routines as Grammars of Action." *Administrative Science Quarterly* 39 (3): 484–510.

Perrow, Charles. 1972. *Complex Organizations.* Glenview, IL: Scott, Foresman.

———. 1986. *Complex Organizations: A Critical Essay.* New York: McGraw-Hill.

Perry, James L., and Wouter Vandenabeele. 2008. "Behavioral Dynamics: Institutions, Identities, and Self Regulation." In *Motivation in Public Management: The Call of Public Service,* edited by James L. Perry and Annie Hondeghem, 56–79. New York: Oxford University Press.

Perry, James L., and Lois Recascino Wise. 1990. "The Motivational Bases of Public Service." *Public Administration Review* 50 (3): 367–73.

Perry, James L., and Hal G. Rainey. 1988. "The Public-Private Distinction in Organization Theory: A Critique and Research Strategy." *Academy of Management Review* 13 (2): 182–201.

Pettit, Philip. 1995. "The Cunning of Trust." *Philosophy and Public Affairs* 24 (3): 202–25.

Polanyi, Michael. 1962. "Tacit Knowing: Its Bearing on Some Problems of Philosophy." *Reviews of Modern Physics* 34 (4): 601.

———. 1967. "Sense-Giving and Sense-Reading." *Philosophy* 42 (162): 301–25.

Porter, Lyman, W., Gregory A. Bigley, and Richard M. Steers. 2003. *Motivation and Work Behaviour*. New York: McGraw-Hill.

Portillo, Shannon. 2012. "The Paradox of Rules: Rules as Resources and Constraints." *Administration and Society* 44 (1): 87–108.

Portillo, Shannon, and Leisha DeHart-Davis. 2009. "Gender and Organizational Rule Abidance." *Public Administration Review* 69 (2): 339–47.

Powell, Walter W., and Paul DiMaggio. 1991. *The New Institutionalism in Organizational Analysis*. 17th ed. Chicago: University of Chicago Press.

Price, Jeffrey C., and Jeffrey S. Forrest. 2016. *Practical Aviation Security: Predicting and Preventing Future Threats*. 3rd ed. Waltham, MA: Butterworth-Heinemann.

Prottas, Jeffrey. 1979. *People Processing: The Street-Level Bureaucrat in Public Service Bureaucracies*. Lexington, KY: Lexington Books.

Pugh, D. S., D. J. Hickson, C. R. Hinings, and C. Turner. 1968. "Dimensions of Organization Structure." *Administrative Science Quarterly* 13 (1): 105.

Raadschelders, J. C. N. 2011. *Public Administration: The Interdisciplinary Study of Government*. New York: Oxford University Press.

Rainey, Hal G. 2014. *Understanding and Managing Public Organizations: Essential Texts for Nonprofit and Public Leadership and Management*. 5th ed. San Francisco, CA: Wiley.

Rainey, Hal G., Sanjay Pandey, and Barry Bozeman. 1995. "Research Note: Public and Private Managers' Perceptions of Red Tape." *Public Administration Review* 55 (6): 567–74.

Rainey, Hal G., and Paula Steinbauer. 1999. "Galloping Elephants: Developing Elements of a Theory of Effective Government Organizations." *Journal of Public Administration Research and Theory* 9 (1): 1–32.

Raven, Bertram H., and John R. P. French Jr. 1958. "Legitimate Power, Coercive Power, and Observability in Social Influence." *Sociometry* 21 (2): 83–97.

Reason, James, Anthony Manstead, Stephen Stradling, James Baxter, and Karen Campbell. 1990. "Errors and Violations on the Roads: A Real Distinction?" *Ergonomics* 33 (10–11): 1315–32.

Reason, James, Dianne Parker, and Rebecca Lawton. 1998. "Organizational Controls and Safety: The Varieties of Rule-Related Behavior." *Journal of Occupational and Organizational Psychology* 71: 289–304.

Reskin, Barbara F., and Debra Branch McBrier. 2000. "Why Not Ascription? Organizations' Employment of Male and Female Managers." *American Sociological Review* 65 (2): 210–33.

Reynaud, Bénédicte. 2002. *Operating Rules in Organizations: Macroeconomic and Microeconomic Analyses*. New York: Palgrave Macmillan.

Riccucci, Norma. 2005. *How Management Matters: Street-Level Bureaucrats and Welfare Reform*. Washington, DC: Georgetown University Press.

———. 2010. *Public Administration: Traditions of Inquiry and Philosophies of Knowledge*. Washington, DC: Georgetown University Press.

Rizzo, John R., Robert J. House, and Sidney I. Lirtzman. 1970. "Role Conflict and Ambiguity in Complex Organizations." *Administrative Science Quarterly* 15 (2): 150–63.

Robbins, Stephen P., and Timothy A. Judge. 2016. *Essentials of Organizational Behavior.* 13th ed. London: Pearson.

Romme, A. G. L., S. van Dijk, H. Berends, M. Jelinek, and M. Weggeman. 2011. "Micro-Institutional Affordances and Strategies of Radical Innovation." *Organization Studies* 32 (11): 1485–1513.

Romzek, Barbara S., and Melvin J. Dubnick. 1987. "Accountability in the Public Sector: Lessons from the *Challenger* Tragedy." *Public Administration Review* 47 (3): 227–38. doi:10.2307/975901.

Rosenbloom, David H., and Rosemary O'Leary. 1997. *Public Administration and Law.* New York: Marcel Dekker.

Roth, Wendy D., and Gerhard Sonnert. 2011. "The Costs and Benefits of 'Red Tape': Anti-Bureaucratic Structure and Gender Inequity in a Science Research Organization." *Social Studies of Science* 41 (3): 385–409.

Rubin, Ellen V. 2009. "The Role of Procedural Justice in Public Personnel Management: Empirical Results from the Department of Defense." *Journal of Public Administration Research and Theory* 19 (1): 125–43.

Rush, Christine L., and J. Edward Kellough. 2015. "Knowledge of Federal EEO Law among County Administrators and Department Heads: Examining the Extent and Determinants of Understanding." Review of Public Personnel Administration Survey, 0734371X15616168. doi:10.1177/0734371X15616168.

Sandfort, Jodi. 2000. "Moving Beyond Discretion and Outcomes: Examining Public Management from the Front Lines of the Welfare System." *Journal of Public Administration Research and Theory* 10 (4): 729–56.

Sandfort, Jodi, and Stephanie Moulton. 2015. *Effective Implementation in Practice: Integrating Public Policy and Management.* Hoboken, NJ: John Wiley & Sons.

Schank, Roger, and Robert Abelson. 1977. *Scripts, Plans, Goals, and Understanding: An Inquiry into Human Knowledge Structures.* Hillsdale, NJ: Lawrence Erlbaum.

Schulz, Martin. 1998. "Limits to Bureaucratic Growth: The Density Dependence of Organizational Rule Births." *Administrative Science Quarterly* 43 (4): 845–76.

———. 2003. "Impermanent Institutionalization: The Duration Dependence of Organizational Rule Changes." *Industrial and Corporate Change* 12 (5): 1077–98.

Scott, Patrick G., and Sanjay K. Pandey. 2000. "The Influence of Red Tape on Bureaucratic Behavior: An Experimental Simulation." *Journal of Policy Analysis and Management* 19 (4): 615–33.

———. 2005. "Red Tape and Public Service Motivation: Findings from a National Survey of Managers in State Health and Human Services Agencies." *Review of Public Personnel Administration* 25 (2): 155–80.

Seeman, Melvin. 1959. "On the Meaning of Alienation." *American Sociological Review* 24 (6): 783–91.

Sekerka, Leslie E., and Roxanne Zolin. 2007. "Rule-Bending: Can Prudential Judgment Affect Rule Compliance and Values in the Workplace?" *Public Integrity* 9 (3): 225–43.

Senigaglia, Cristiana. 2011. "Max Weber and the Parliamentary Bureaucracy of His Time." *Parliaments, Estates, and Representation* 31 (1): 53–66.

Sidney, G. W. 1987. "Knowledge and Competence as Strategic Assets." In *The Competitive Challenge: Strategies for Industrial Innovation and Renewal,* edited by D. J. Teese, 159–84. Cambridge, MA: Ballinger.

Sil, Rudra, and Peter J. Katzenstein. 2011. "De-Centering, Not Discarding, the "isms": Some Friendly Amendments." *International Studies Quarterly* 55 (2): 481–85.

Sitkin, Sim B. 1995. "On the Positive Effects of Legalization on Trust." *Research on Negotiation in Organizations* 5: 185–218.

Simon, Herbert Alexander. 1947. *Administrative Behavior: A Study of Decision-Making Processes in Administrative Organization.* London: Macmillan.

Sitkin, Sim B., and Robert J. Bies. 1993. "The Legalistic Organization: Definitions, Dimensions, and Dilemmas." *Organization Science* 4 (3): 345–51.

———. 1994. *The Legalistic Organization.* New York: SAGE.

Staw, Barry M., and Richard D. Boettger. 1990. "Task Revision: A Neglected Form of Work Performance." *Academy of Management Journal* 33 (3): 534–59.

Stinchcombe, Arthur L. 2001. *When Formality Works: Authority and Abstraction in Law and Organizations.* Chicago: University of Chicago Press.

Stivers, Camilla. 2002. *Gender Images in Public Administration.* 2nd ed. Cleveland, OH: Cleveland State University.

———. 2008. *Governance in Dark Times: Practical Philosophy for Public Service.* Washington, DC: Georgetown University Press.

Stone, Clarence N., and Eleanor G. Feldbaum. 1976. "Blame, Complacency, and Pessimism: Attitudes and Problem Perceptions among Selected Street Level Administrators in Two Suburban Counties." *Administration and Society* 8 (1): 79–106.

Stryker, Robin. 2000. "Legitimacy Processes as Institutional Politics: Implications for Theory and Research in the Sociology of Organizations." In *Research in the Sociology of Organizations,* vol. 17, edited by Michael Lounsbury, 179–223. Bingley, UK: Emerald Group.

Suchman, Mark C. 1995. "Managing Legitimacy: Strategic and Institutional Approaches" *Academy of Management Review* 20 (3): 571–610.

Sutcliffe, Kathleen M., and Gerry McNamara. 2001. "Controlling Decision Making Practice in Organizations." *Organization Science* 12: 484. http://go.galegroup.com .libproxy.lib.unc.edu/ps/i.do?id=GALE%7CA90570115&v=2.1&u=unc_main &it=r&p=AONE&sw=w.

Terman, Jessica. 2013. "Evaluating Political Signals: The Nature of Bureaucratic Response in Minority Preference Purchasing." *American Review of Public Administration* 44 (5): 522–49.

———. 2016. "What Happens When Rules Stay the Same? Examining Changes in

Implementation Intent Over Time." *International Journal of Public Administration* (online) at http://dx.doi.org/10.1080/01900692.2015.1072555, 1–18.

Thibaut, John W., and Laurens Walker. 1975. *Procedural Justice: A Psychological Analysis.* Hillsdale, NJ: Lawrence Erlbaum.

Thompson, E. P. 1967. "Time, Work-Discipline, and Industrial Capitalism." *Past and Present* 38: 56–97.

Thompson, Victor. 1961. *Modern Organization.* New York: Alfred A Knopf.

———. 1977. *Modern Organization.* 2nd ed. Tuscaloosa: University of Alabama Press.

Tolbert, Pamela, and Richard Hall. 2009. *Organizations: Structures, Processes, and Outcomes.* 10th ed. Upper Saddle River, NJ: Pearson/Prentice Hall.

Tsoukas, H., and E. Vladimirou. 2001. "What Is Organizational Knowledge?" *Journal of Management Studies* 38 (7): 973–93.

Tummers, Lars. 2011. "Explaining the Willingness of Public Professionals to Implement New Policies: A Policy Alienation Framework." *International Review of Administrative Sciences* 77 (3): 555–81.

———. 2012. "Policy Alienation of Public Professionals: The Construct and Its Measurement." *Public Administration Review* 72 (4): 516–25.

Tummers, Lars L.G., Victor Bekkers, Evelien Vink, and Michael Musheno. 2015. "Coping during Public Service Delivery: A Conceptualization and Systematic Review of the Literature." *Journal of Public Administration Research and Theory* 25 (4): 1099–26.

Tummers, Lars, and Eva Knies. 2014. "The Public Leadership Questionnaire: The Development and Validation of Five Dimensions of Public Leadership Behaviors." *International Research Society for Public Management (IRSPM).* Retrieved from http://hdl.handle.net/1765/51018.

Tummers, Lars, Bram Steijn, and Victor Bekkers. 2012. "Explaining the Willingness of Public Professionals to Implement Public Policies: Content, Context, and Personality Characteristics." *Public Administration* 90 (3): 716–36.

Tummers, Lars L.G., Ulrike Weske, Robin Bouwman, and Stephan G. Grimmelikhuijsen. 2015. "The Impact of Red Tape on Citizen Satisfaction: An Experimental Study." *International Public Management Journal* 19 (3): 320–41.

Tyler, Tom R. 1989. "The Psychology of Procedural Justice: A Test of the Group-Value Model." *Journal of Personality and Social Psychology* 57 (5): 830–38.

———. 2001. "Public Trust and Confidence in Legal Authorities: What Do Majority and Minority Group Members Want from the Law and Legal Institutions?" *Behavioral Sciences and the Law* 19 (2): 215–35.

———. 2003. "Trust within Organisations." *Personnel Review* 32 (5): 556–68.

———. 2006. "Psychological Perspectives on Legitimacy and Legitimation." *Annual Review of Psychology* 57 (1): 375–400.

Tyler, Tom, and Steven Blader. 2000. *Cooperation in Groups: Procedural Justice, Social Identity, and Behavioral Engagement.* Philadelphia: Taylor & Francis.

———. 2005. "Can Businesses Effectively Regulate Employee Conduct? The Antecedents of Rule Following in Work Settings." *Academy of Management Journal* 48 (6): 1143–58.

Tyler, Tom R., and E. A. Lind. 1992. "A Relational Model of Authority in Groups." *Advances in Experimental Social Psychology* 25: 115–91.

US Department of Labor (DOL). 1922. *National War Labor Board: A History of Its Formation and Activities, Together with Its Awards and the Documents of Importance in the Record of Its Development.* Washington, DC: Government Printing Office.

US National Performance Review. 1993. *From Red Tape to Results: Creating a Government that Works Better and Costs Less.* Washington, DC: Government Printing Office.

Vandenabeele, Wouter. 2007. "Toward a Public Administration Theory of Public Service Motivation." *Public Management Review* 9 (4): 545–56.

Van der Wal, Zeger, Gjalt De Graaf, and Karin Lasthuizen. 2008. "What's Valued Most? Similarities and Differences between the Organizational Values of the Public and Private Sector." *Public Administration* 86 (2): 465–82.

Van Wart, Montgomery. 1998. *Changing Public Sector Values.* New York: Garland.

van Witteloostuijn, Arjen, and Gjalt de Jong. 2009. "Ecology of National Rule Birth: A Longitudinal Study of Dutch Higher Education Law, 1960–2004." *Journal of Public Administration Research and Theory* 20 (1): 187–213.

Vardi, Yoav, and Ely Weitz. 2004. *Misbehavior in Organizations: Theory, Research, and Management.* Mahwah, NJ: Lawrence Erlbaum.

Vrij, Aldert. 2008. *Detecting Lies and Deceit: Pitfalls and Opportunities.* Hoboken, NJ: John Wiley.

Vlaar, Paul W. L., Frans A. J. Van den Bosch, and H. W. Volberda. 2006. "Coping with Problems of Understanding in Interorganizational Relationships: Using Formalization as a Means to Make Sense." *Organization Studies* 27 (11): 1617–38.

———. 2007. "Towards a Dialectic Perspective on Formalization in Interorganizational Relationships: How Alliance Managers Capitalize on the Duality Inherent in Contracts, Rules, and Procedures." *Organization Studies* 28 (4): 437–66.

Walker, Richard M., and Gene A. Brewer. 2008. "An Organizational Echelon Analysis of the Determinants of Red Tape in Public Organizations." *Public Administration Review* 68 (6): 1112–27.

Watkins-Hayes, Celeste. 2011. "Race, Respect, and Red Tape: Inside the Black Box of Racially Representative Bureaucracies." *Journal of Public Administration Research and Theory* 21 (supplement 2): i251.

Weber, Max. 1946. *From Max Weber: Essays in Sociology.* Translated by H. H. Gerth and C. Wright Mills. New York: Oxford University Press.

———. 1947. *The Theory of Economic and Social Organization.* Translated by A. M. Henderson and Talcott Parsons. New York: Oxford University Press.

———. 2012. *The Protestant Ethic and the Spirit of Capitalism.* Translated by Talcott Parsons. Minneola, NY: Dover.

———. 2013. *From Max Weber: Essays in Sociology.* New York: Routledge.

Weber, Max, Guenther Roth, and Clause Wittich. 1978. *Economy and Society: An Outline of Interpretive Sociology.* Berkeley: University of California Press.

Wenger, Jeffrey B., and Vicky M. Wilkins. 2009. "At the Discretion of Rogue Agents:

How Automation Improves Women's Outcomes in Unemployment Insurance." *Journal of Public Administration Research and Theory* 19 (2): 313–33.

Whitener, Ellen M., Susan E. Brodt, M. Audrey Korsgaard, and Jon M. Werner. 1998. "Managers as Initiators of Trust: An Exchange Relationship Framework for Understanding Managerial Trustworthy Behavior." *Academy of Management Review* 23 (3): 513–30.

Wilson, James. 1989. *Bureaucracy: What Government Agencies Do and Why They Do It.* New York: Basic.

Winter, Sidney. 1987. "Knowledge and Competence as Strategic Assets." In *The Competitive Challenge: Strategies for Industrial Innovation and Renewal,* edited by D. J. Teece, 159–84. Cambridge, MA: Ballinger.

Wise, Lois Recascino. 2004. "Bureaucratic Posture: On the Need for a Composite Theory of Bureaucratic Behavior." *Public Administration Review* 64 (6): 669–80. doi:10.1111/j.1540-6210.2004.00414.x.

Wittgenstein, Ludwig. 2010. *Philosophical Investigations.* 4th ed. Chicester, UK: John Wiley & Sons.

Yenney, Sharon L. 1977. "In Defense of Grievance Procedure in a Non-Union Setting." *Employee Relations Law Journal* 2 (4): 434–43.

Young v. United Parcel Service, Inc. 2015. 1226, 12, US Court of Appeals for the Fourth Circuit, 707 F. 3d, 437.

Zollo, Maurizo, and Sidney G. Winter. 2002. "Deliberate Learning and the Evolution of Dynamic Capabilities." *Organization Science* 13 (3): 339–51.

INDEX

Figures and tables are denoted by f and t following the page number.

grievance policies: in behavioral perspective, 99–102; constraint and, 93, 95–96; empowerment and, 93, 95–96; goals of, 92; in individual perspective, 95–99; knowledge capacity and, 93–94; legitimacy and, 94, 98; malicious compliance and, 101–2; norms and, 94–95; in organizational perspective, 92–95; organizational rules framework and, 91–103; restraint and, 93; retaliation and, 100–101; risk and, 92, 95, 103n4; socialization and, 94; status-leveling and, 96–97; trust and, 99; values and, 94–95; workplace conflict and, 92–93
group identity theory, 49
Gulick, Luther, 118
Guy, Mary, 15

Hage, Jerald, 72
Haraway, William, 100, 101
HB2. *See* Public Facilities Privacy and Security Act (North Carolina)
Herd, Pamela, 141
historical preservation, as public value, 9*t*
honesty, as public value, 9*t*

inconsistent application, of rules, 49–50, 49*t*, 56*f*, 117–18
individual perspective, 91, 136, 137*t*; constraint in, 41–44, 45*f*; empowerment in, 41–44, 45*f*; as experience, 41; grievance policies in, 95–99; legitimacy in, 45–47, 59n3, 98; organizational identification in, 57–58, 58*f*; procedural fairness in, 47–50, 48*f*, 49*t*, 97–98; status-leveling in, 50–53, 96–97; trust in, 53–57, 54*f*, 56*f*, 99
integrity, as public value, 9*t*
intent, in rule violations, 69
interaction, 106–7
interpretation, rule, 62, 63*f*, 64

Jacobson, Willow, 30
Jakobsen, Mads, 142
Jørgensen, Torben, 9
Jos, Philip, 32
judgment, rule behavior and, 86–88, 139*t*

Kaufman, Herbert, 13
Kellough, Edward, 51
Kirby, Erika, 32
knowledge: codification of, 34; in organizational perspective, 33–37
Krone, Kathleen, 32

Lawton, Rebecca, 81
learning, in organizational perspective, 33–37
learning, organizational, 107
legalism: legitimacy and, 38; overcontrol and, 133n3; as public value, 9*t*
legal-rational authority, 23
legitimacy: accountability and, 28, 132; authority and, 45, 81–84, 139*t*; formalization and, 114–15; grievance policies and, 94, 98; in individual perspective, 45–47, 59n3, 98; in organizational perspective, 37–38; rule behavior and, 81–84, 139*t*
Leventhal, Gerald, 47
Lewin, David, 96–97
LGWS. *See* Local Government Workplaces Study (LGWS)
Lipsky, Michael, 13–14
Local Government Workplaces Study (LGWS), 15–16, 21, 24, 24*f*, 26, 26*f*, 29, 30, 30*f*, 35–36, 44, 45*f*, 46, 48*f*, 49*t*, 51, 54*f*, 56*f*, 58*f*, 61, 65–66, 65*f*, 70*f*, 71, 73*f*, 75, 76, 76*f*, 81, 83, 86, 87–88, 92, 104n4, 107–8, 112, 113, 119–20, 120*f*, 122, 122*f*, 128, 128*f*, 140, 145–48, 147*t*
logic: of appropriateness, 80–81; formal, 35; rule, 116
Loy, James, 116

ABOUT THE AUTHOR

Leisha DeHart-Davis is an Albert and Gladys Coates Distinguished Term Associate Professor at the School of Government at the University of North Carolina–Chapel Hill. She studies public organizational behavior and diversity. Her articles have appeared in the *Journal of Public Administration Research and Theory, Public Administration Review, International Public Management Journal, Administration and Society,* and *Review of Public Personnel Administration.*

CPSIA information can be obtained
at www.ICGtesting.com
Printed in the USA
BVOW11s0242120517
483933BV00003B/5/P